This Book Belong To:

_____

_____

_____

_____

_____

Date: _____ Time: _____

Location: _____

Weather Conditions

☀ ☁ ⛅ 🌧 🌧 🌨 🚩 🌡
☐ ☐ ☐ ☐ ☐ ☐ _____ _____

Firearm:	
Bullet:	Seating Depth:
Powder:	Grains:
Primer:	
Brass:	
Distance:	

Overall Results

☐ Poor   ☐ Fair   ☐ Good   ☐ Excellent

Notes

_____
_____
_____

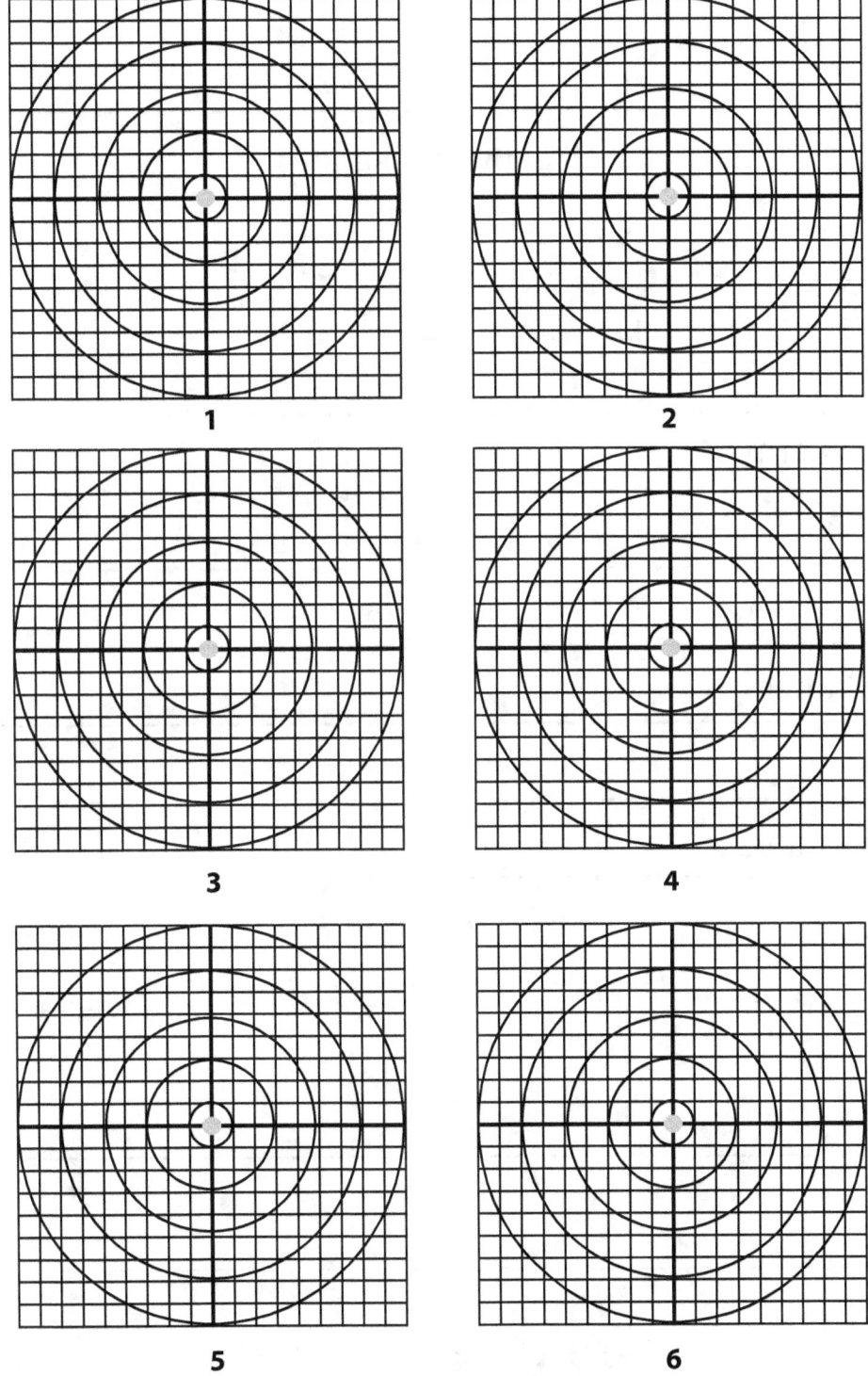

📅 Date: _____ 🕐 Time: _____

📍 Location: _____

Weather Conditions

☀️ ☁️ ⛅ 🌦️ 🌧️ 🌨️ 🚩 _____ 🌡️ _____

☐ ☐ ☐ ☐ ☐ ☐

Firearm:	
Bullet:	Seating Depth:
Powder:	Grains:
Primer:	
Brass:	
Distance:	

Overall Results

☐ Poor ☐ Fair ☐ Good ☐ Excellent

Notes

_____

_____

_____

☆ ☆ ☆ ☆ ☆

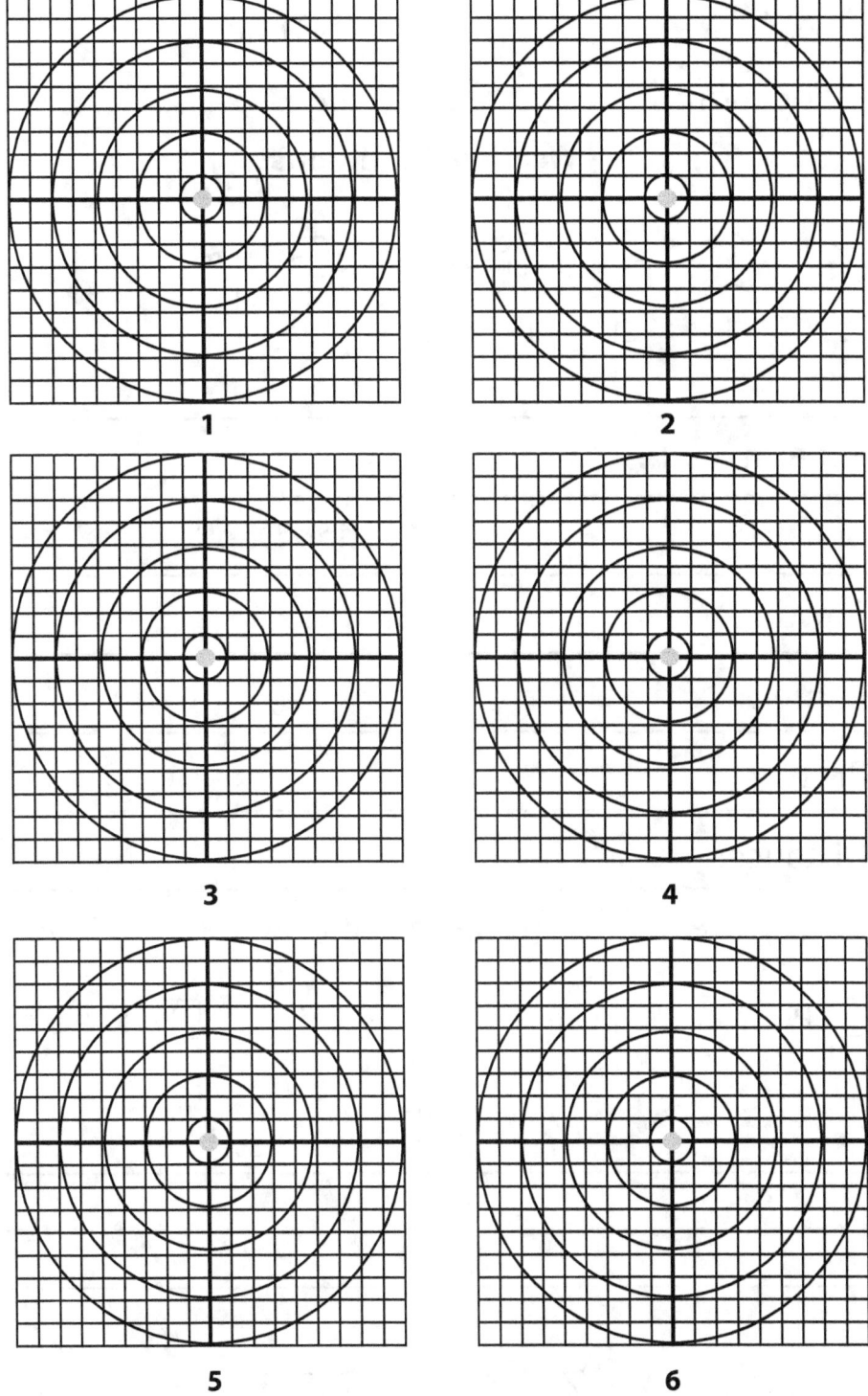

📅 Date: _____   🕐 Time: _____

📍 Location: _____

Weather Conditions

☀️ ☁️ 🌤️ 🌧️ 🌧️ 🌨️ 🚩 🌡️
☐   ☐   ☐   ☐   ☐   ☐   ____ ____

Firearm:	
Bullet:	Seating Depth:
Powder:	Grains:
Primer:	
Brass:	
Distance:	

Overall Results

☐ Poor   ☐ Fair   ☐ Good   ☐ Excellent

Notes

_____

_____

_____

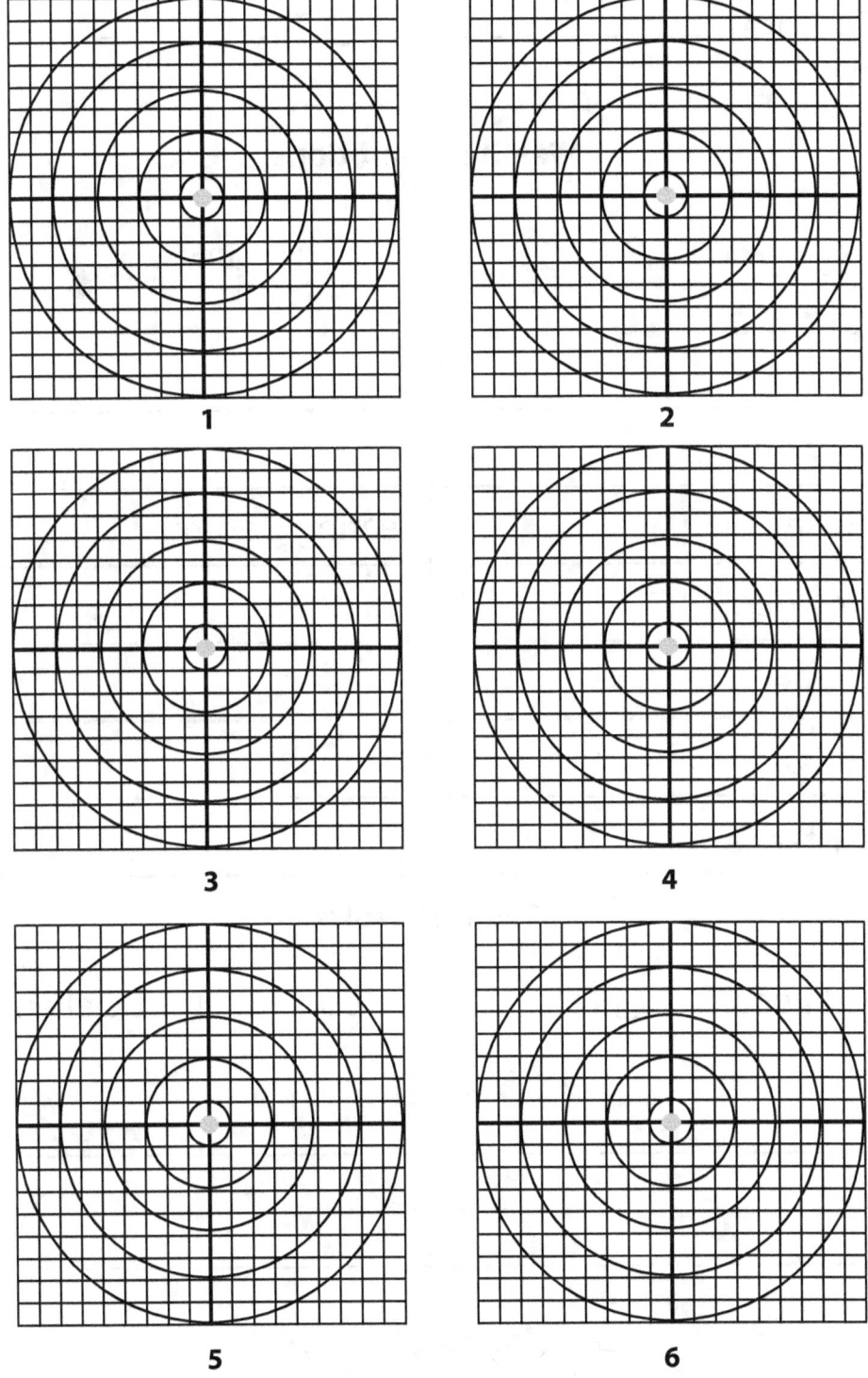

📅 Date: _____ 🕐 Time: _____

📍 Location: _____

Weather Conditions

☀ ☁ ⛅ 🌧 🌧 🌨 🚩  🌡
☐ ☐ ☐ ☐ ☐ ☐ ☐ ☐

Firearm:	
Bullet:	Seating Depth:
Powder:	Grains:
Primer:	
Brass:	
Distance:	

Overall Results

☐ Poor ☐ Fair ☐ Good ☐ Excellent

Notes

_____
_____
_____

☆ ☆ ☆ ☆ ☆

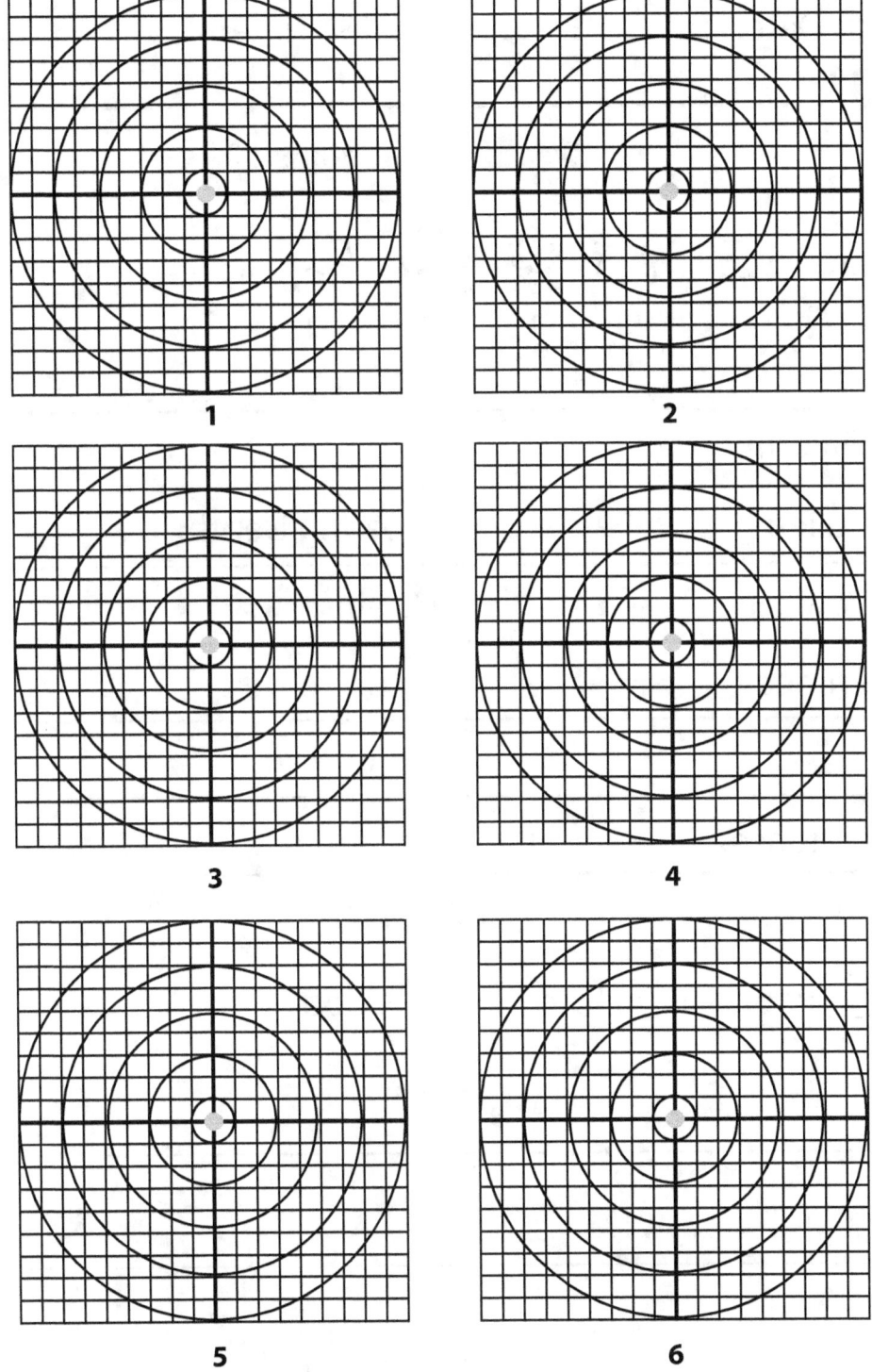

📅 Date: _____ 🕐 Time: _____

📍 Location: _____

Weather Conditions

☀️ ☁️ ⛅ 🌦️ 🌧️ 🌨️ 🚩 🌡️
☐ ☐ ☐ ☐ ☐ ☐ ____ ____

Firearm:	
Bullet:	Seating Depth:
Powder:	Grains:
Primer:	
Brass:	
Distance:	

Overall Results

☐ Poor   ☐ Fair   ☐ Good   ☐ Excellent

Notes

_____

_____

_____

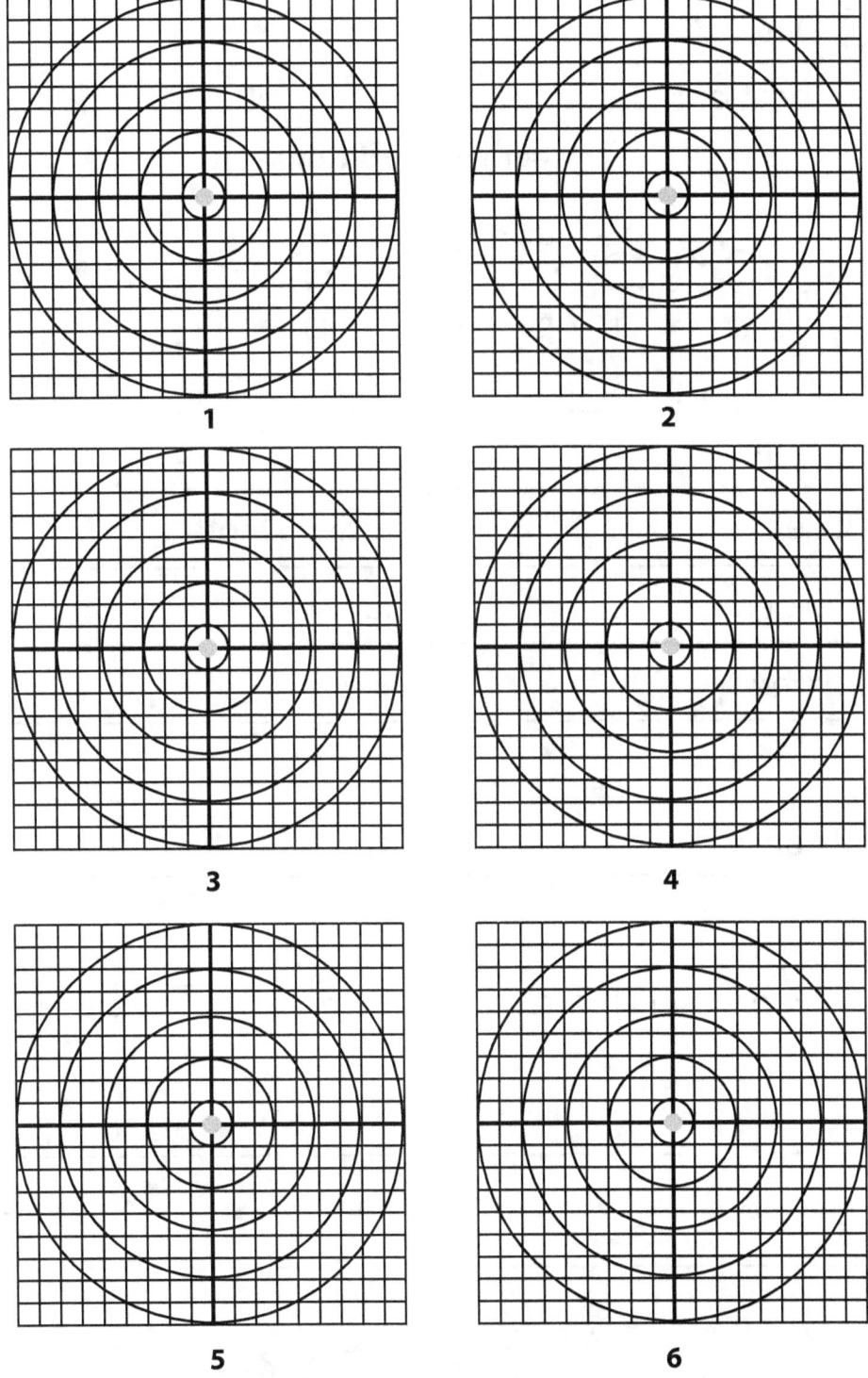

📅 Date: _____ 🕐 Time: _____

📍 Location: _____

Weather Conditions

☀️ ☁️ ⛅ 🌦️ 🌧️ 🌨️ 🚩 🌡️
☐   ☐   ☐   ☐   ☐   ☐   ____ ____

Firearm:	
Bullet:	Seating Depth:
Powder:	Grains:
Primer:	
Brass:	
Distance:	

Overall Results

☐ Poor   ☐ Fair   ☐ Good   ☐ Excellent

Notes

_____

_____

_____

☆ ☆ ☆ ☆ ☆

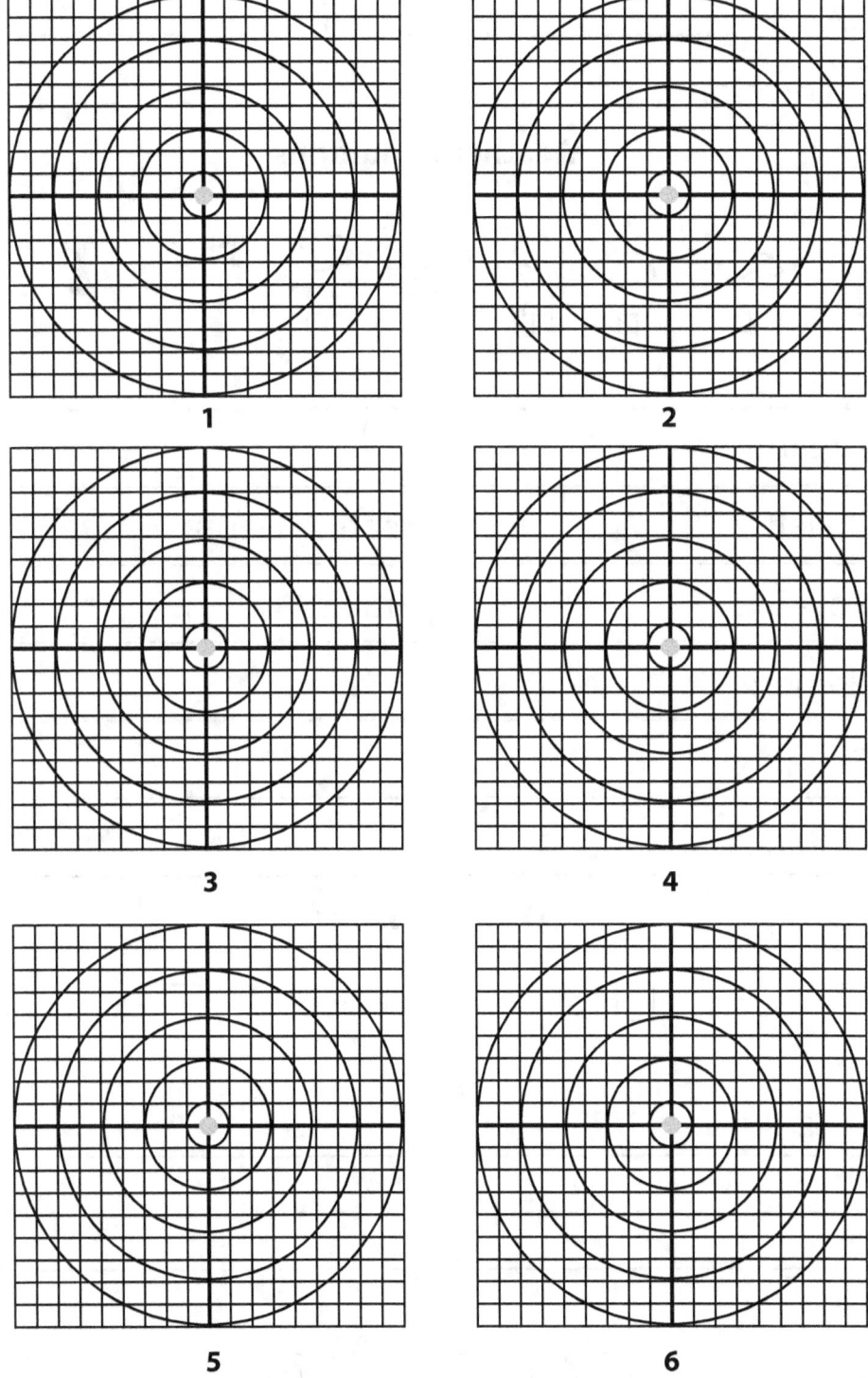

📅 Date: _____ 🕐 Time: _____

📍 Location: _____

Weather Conditions

☀ ☁ ⛅ 🌧 🌧 🌨 🚩 🌡
☐ ☐ ☐ ☐ ☐ ☐

Firearm:	
Bullet:	Seating Depth:
Powder:	Grains:
Primer:	
Brass:	
Distance:	

Overall Results

☐ Poor　　☐ Fair　　☐ Good　　☐ Excellent

Notes

_____
_____
_____

☆ ☆ ☆ ☆ ☆

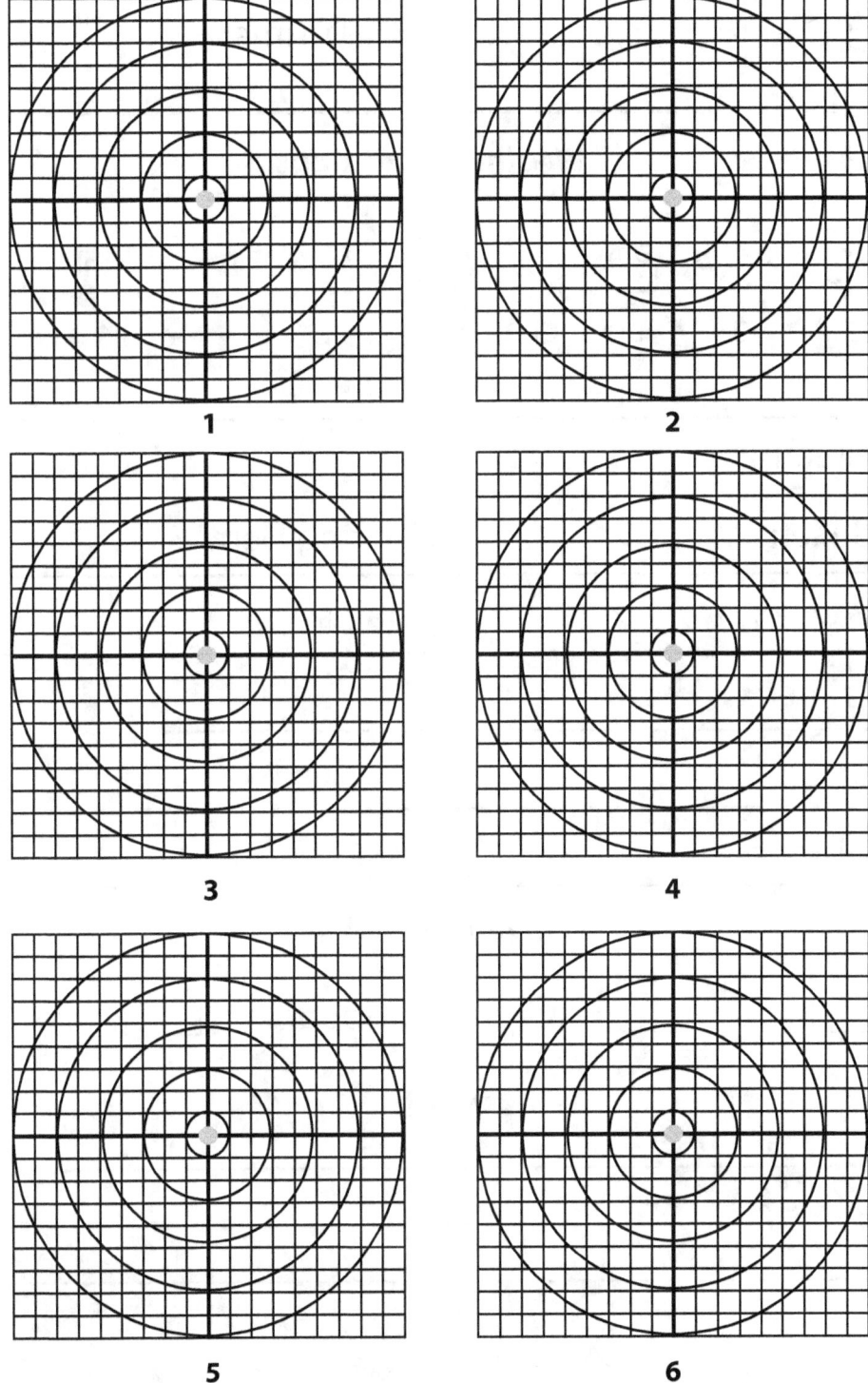

📅 Date: _____ 🕐 Time: _____

📍 Location: _____

Weather Conditions

☀ ☁ ⛅ 🌥 🌧 🌨 🚩 🌡
☐   ☐   ☐   ☐   ☐   ☐   _____   _____

Firearm:	
Bullet:	Seating Depth:
Powder:	Grains:
Primer:	
Brass:	
Distance:	

Overall Results

☐ Poor   ☐ Fair   ☐ Good   ☐ Excellent

Notes

_____
_____
_____

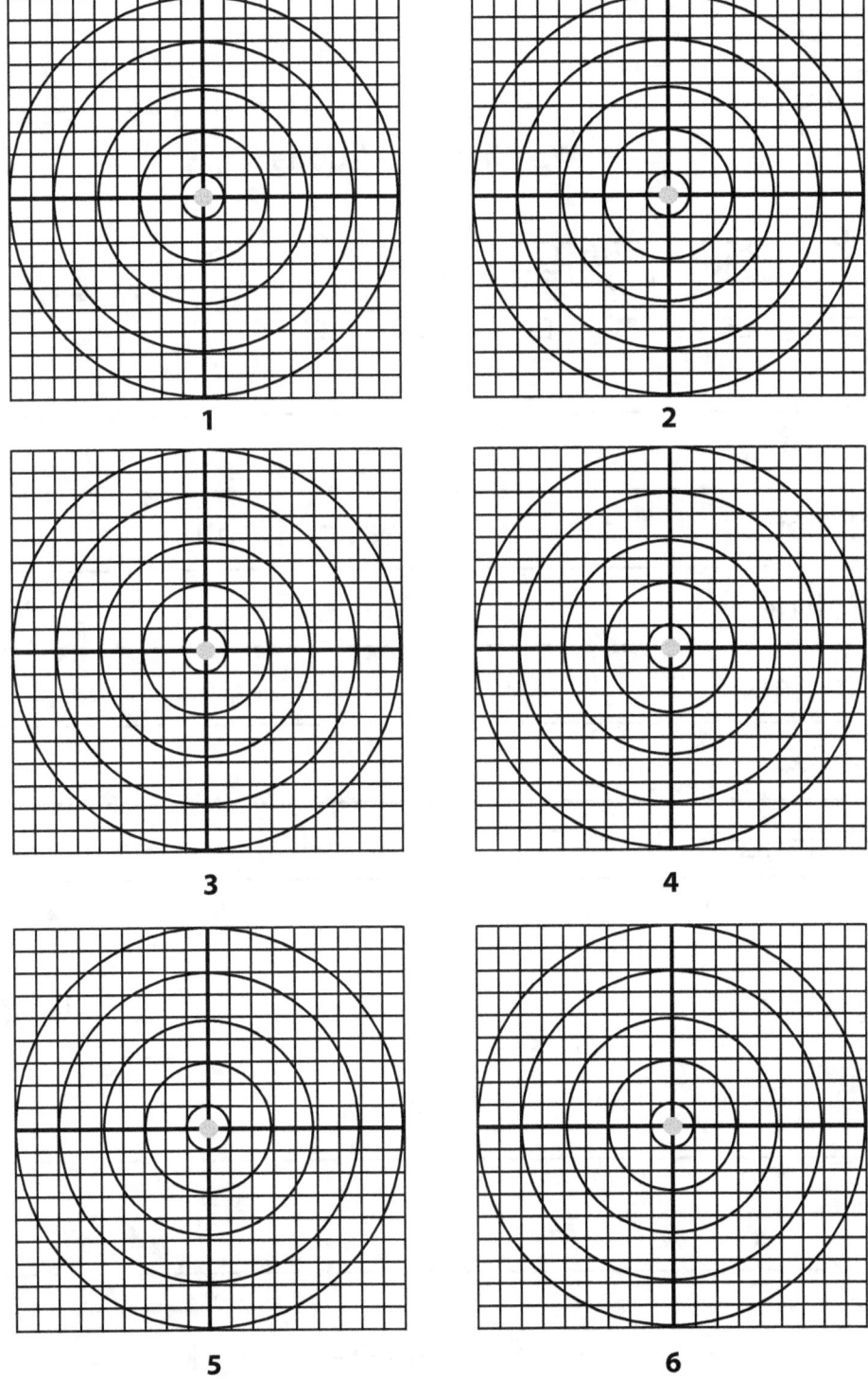

📅 Date: _____ 🕐 Time: _____

📍 Location: _____

Weather Conditions

☀ ☐ ⛅ ☐ 🌤 ☐ 🌦 ☐ ☁ ☐ 🌧 ☐ 🚩 _____ 🌡 _____

Firearm:	
Bullet:	Seating Depth:
Powder:	Grains:
Primer:	
Brass:	
Distance:	

Overall Results

☐ Poor   ☐ Fair   ☐ Good   ☐ Excellent

Notes

_____

_____

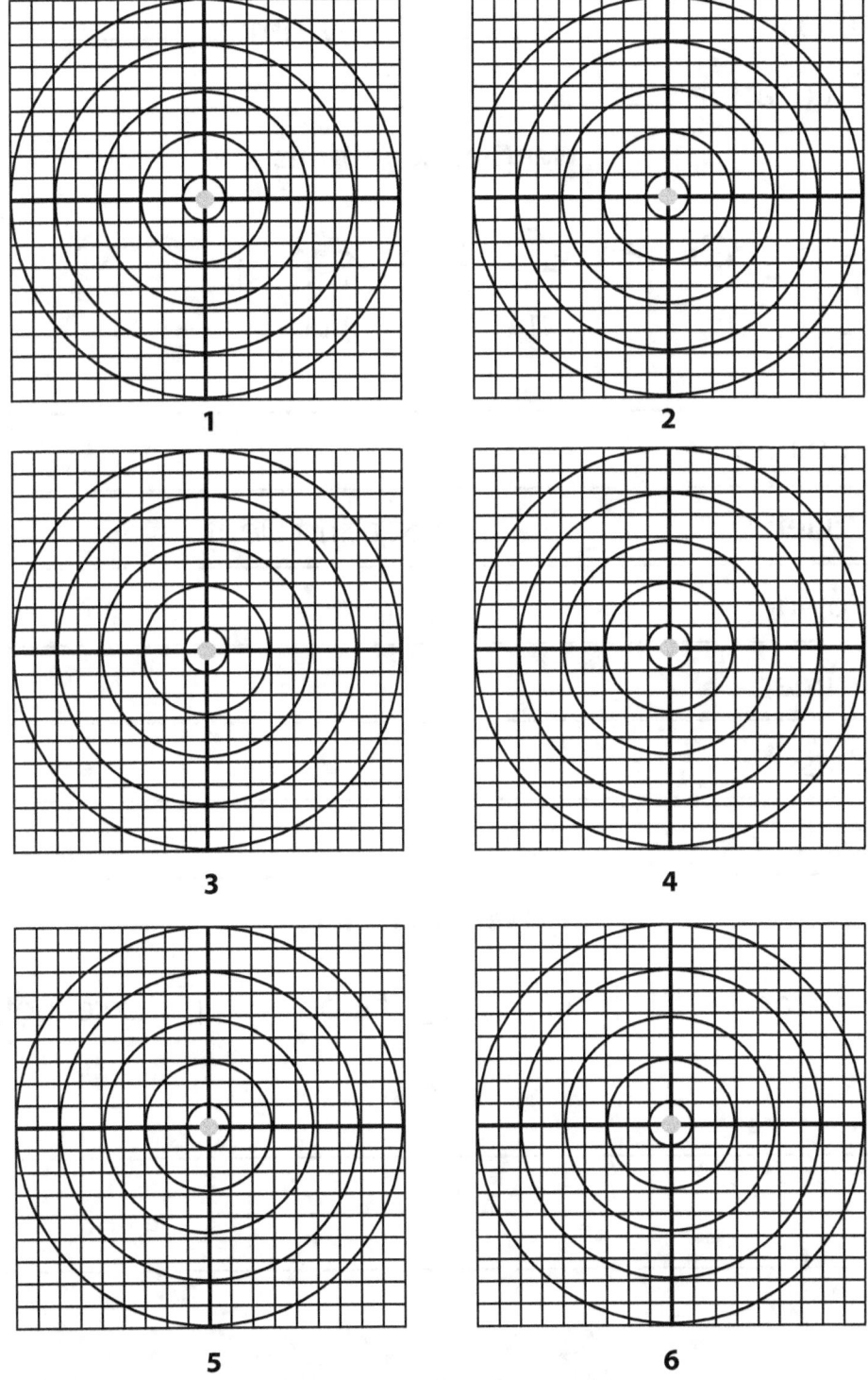

📅 Date: _____ 🕐 Time: _____

📍 Location: _____

Weather Conditions

☀️ ⛅ 🌥️ 🌧️ 🌧️ 🌨️ 🚩 🌡️
☐   ☐   ☐   ☐   ☐   ☐

Firearm:	
Bullet:	Seating Depth:
Powder:	Grains:
Primer:	
Brass:	
Distance:	

Overall Results

☐ Poor   ☐ Fair   ☐ Good   ☐ Excellent

Notes

_____

_____

☆ ☆ ☆ ☆ ☆

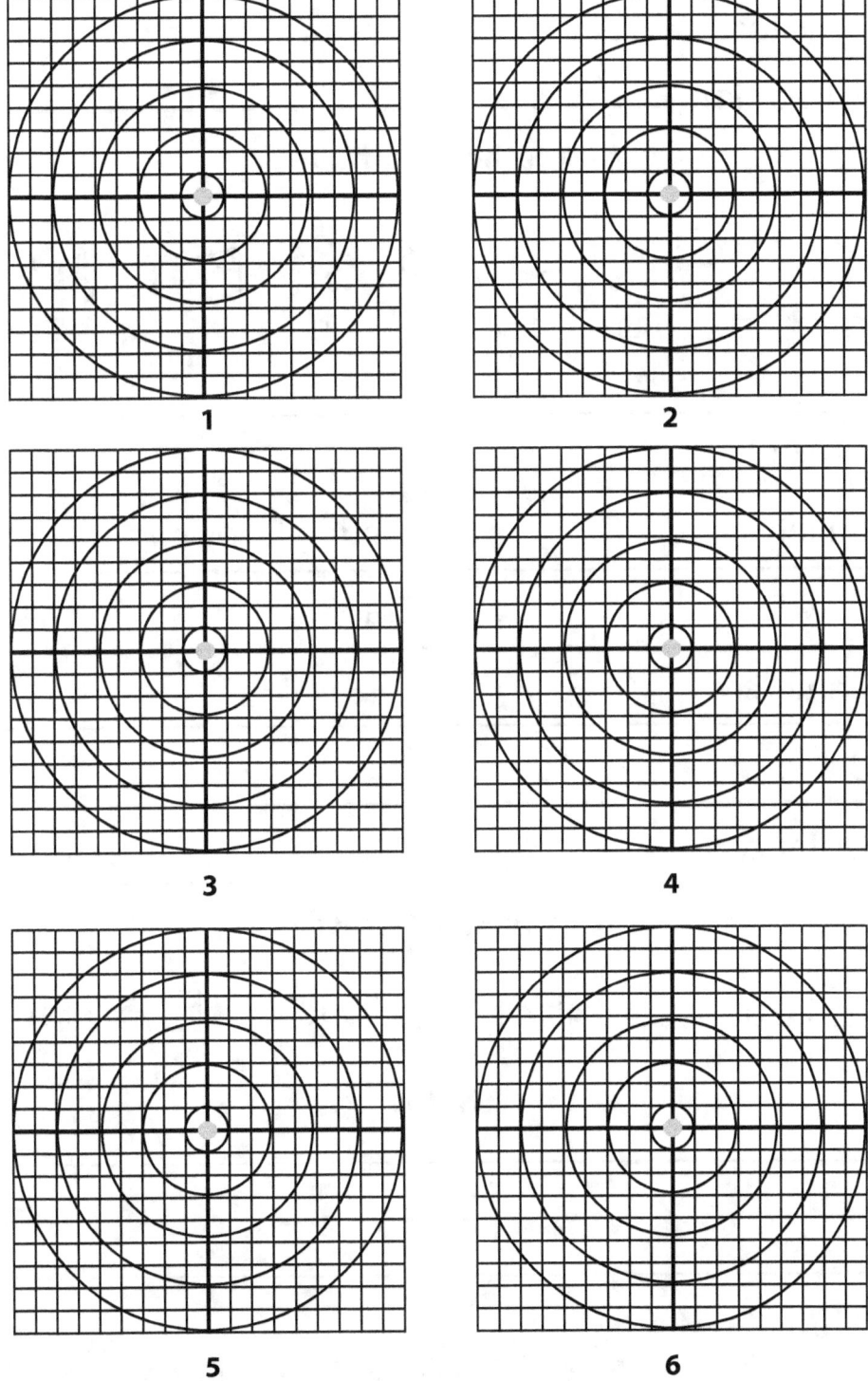

📅 Date: _____ 🕐 Time: _____

📍 Location: _____

Weather Conditions

☀️ ☁️ 🌤️ 🌥️ 🌦️ 🌧️ 🚩 _____ 🌡️ _____
☐   ☐   ☐   ☐   ☐   ☐

Firearm:	
Bullet:	Seating Depth:
Powder:	Grains:
Primer:	
Brass:	
Distance:	

Overall Results

☐ Poor   ☐ Fair   ☐ Good   ☐ Excellent

Notes

_____

_____

_____

☆ ☆ ☆ ☆ ☆

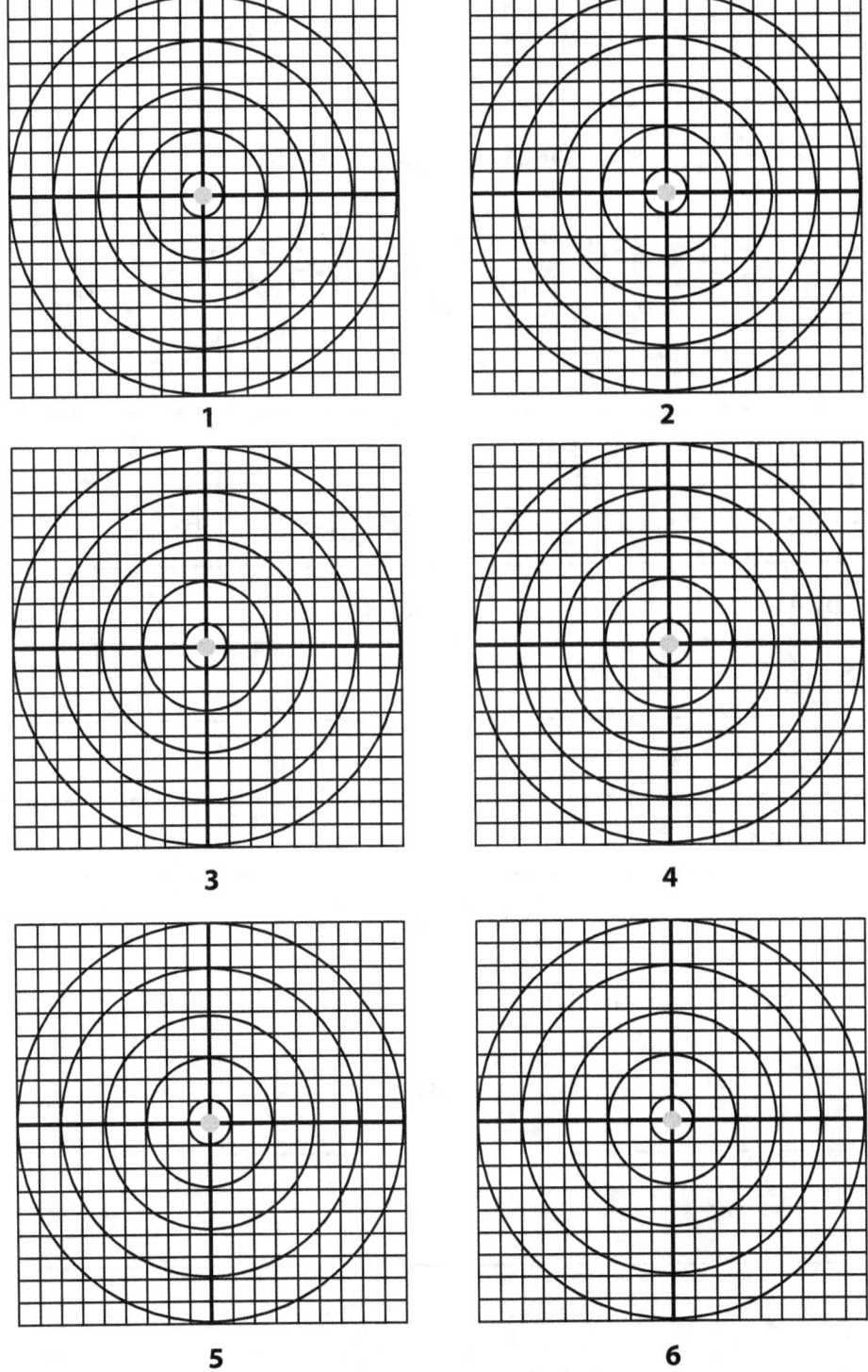

📅 Date: _____ 🕐 Time: _____

📍 Location: _____

Weather Conditions

☀️ ☁️ ⛅ 🌦️ 🌧️ 🌨️ 🚩 🌡️ _____

☐ ☐ ☐ ☐ ☐ ☐

Firearm:	
Bullet:	Seating Depth:
Powder:	Grains:
Primer:	
Brass:	
Distance:	

Overall Results

☐ Poor ☐ Fair ☐ Good ☐ Excellent

Notes

_____

_____

_____

☆ ☆ ☆ ☆ ☆

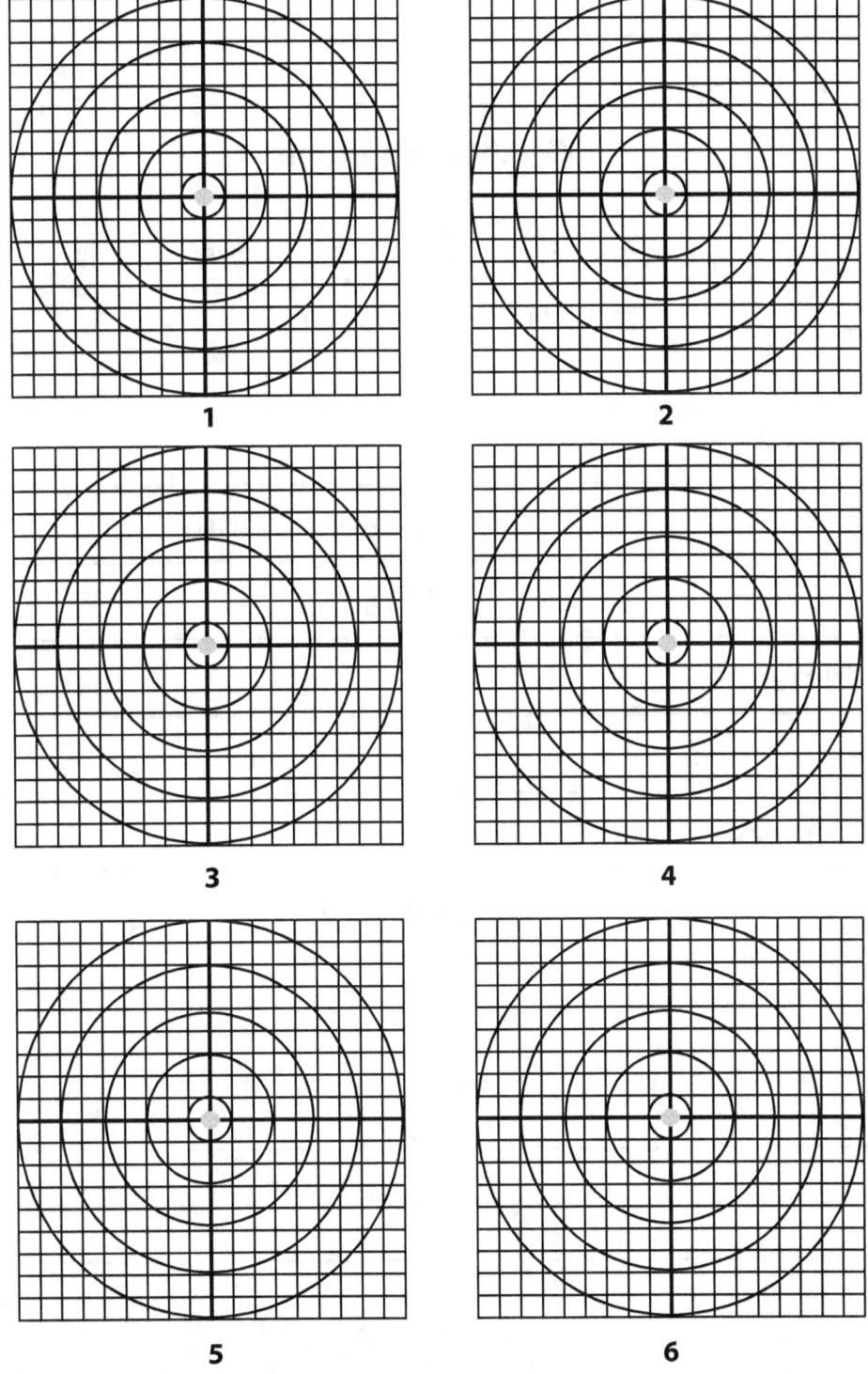

Date: _____ Time: _____

 Location: _____

Weather Conditions

☀ ☁ ⛅ 🌧 🌧 🌨 🚩 🌡
☐ ☐ ☐ ☐ ☐ ☐ ___ ___

Firearm:	
Bullet:	Seating Depth:
Powder:	Grains:
Primer:	
Brass:	
Distance:	

Overall Results

☐ Poor   ☐ Fair   ☐ Good   ☐ Excellent

Notes

_____

_____

☆ ☆ ☆ ☆ ☆

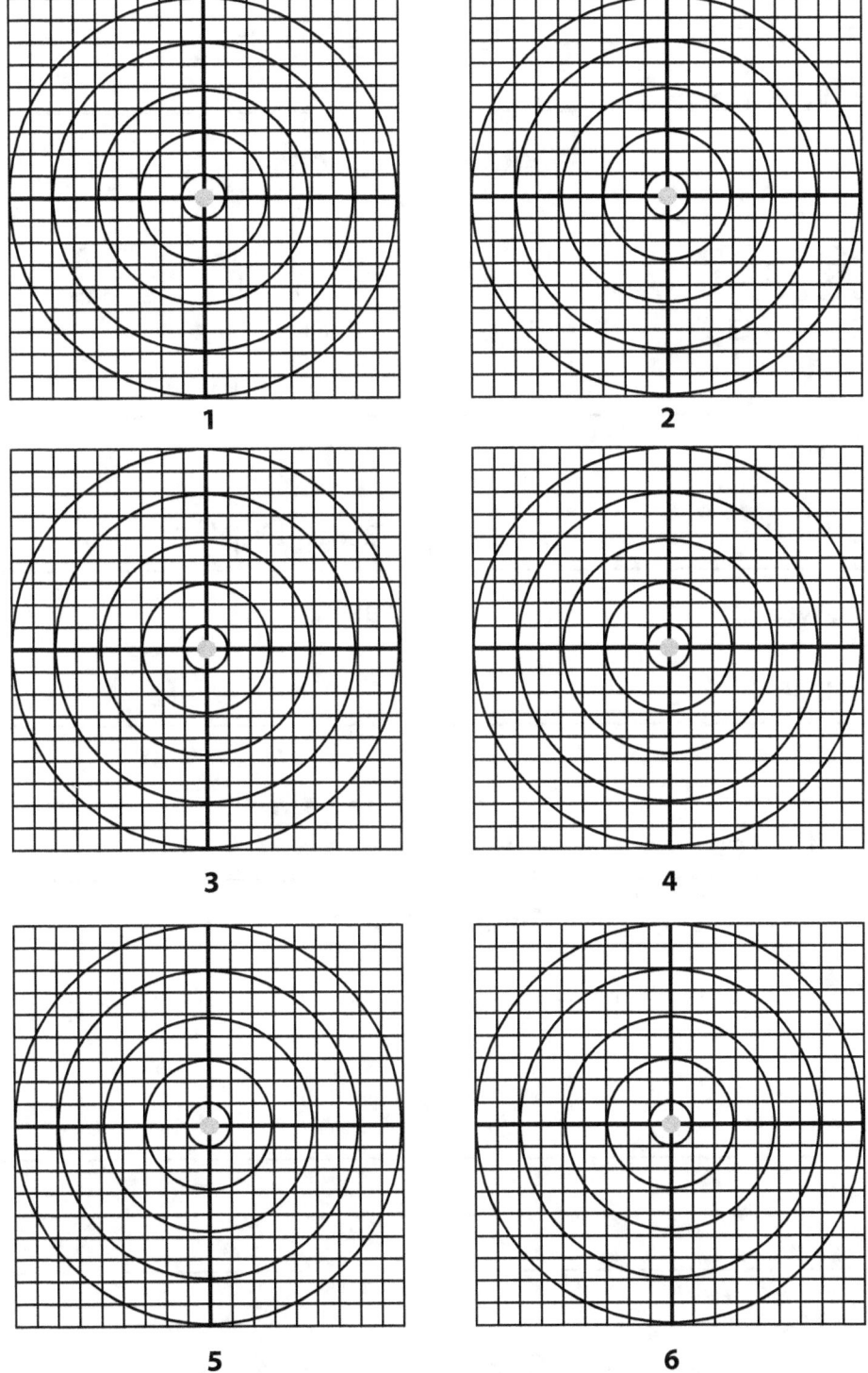

Date: _____   ⏰ Time: _____
 Location: _____

Weather Conditions

☀️ ☁️ 🌤️ 🌧️ 🌦️ 🌨️ 🚩 🌡️ _____
☐   ☐   ☐   ☐   ☐   ☐

Firearm:	
Bullet:	Seating Depth:
Powder:	Grains:
Primer:	
Brass:	
Distance:	

Overall Results

☐ Poor   ☐ Fair   ☐ Good   ☐ Excellent

Notes

_____
_____
_____

☆ ☆ ☆ ☆ ☆

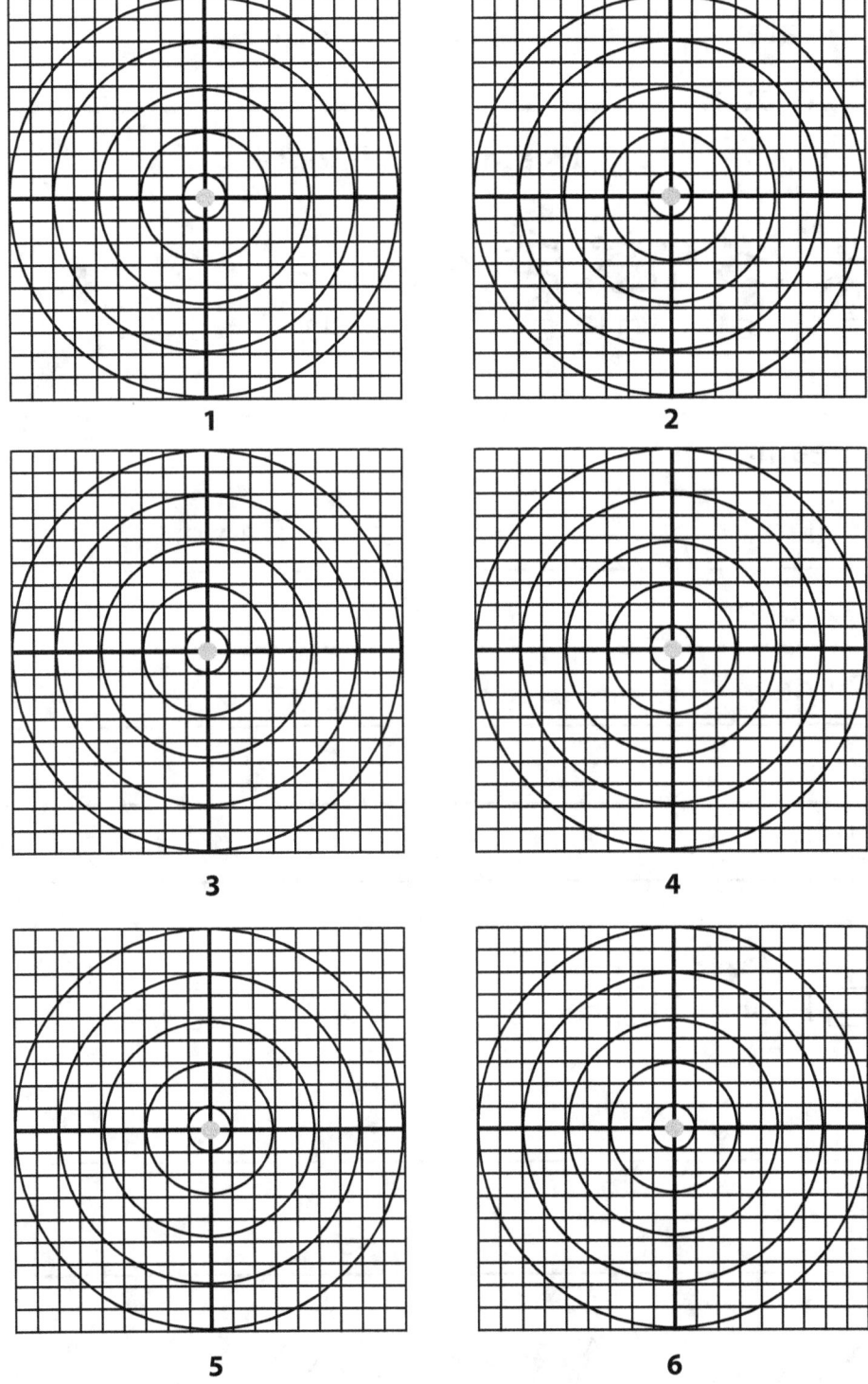

📅 Date: _____ 🕐 Time: _____

📍 Location: _____

Weather Conditions

☀ ☁ ⛅ 🌧 🌧 🌨 🚩 🌡
☐   ☐   ☐   ☐   ☐   ☐

Firearm:	
Bullet:	Seating Depth:
Powder:	Grains:
Primer:	
Brass:	
Distance:	

Overall Results

☐ Poor   ☐ Fair   ☐ Good   ☐ Excellent

Notes

_____

_____

_____

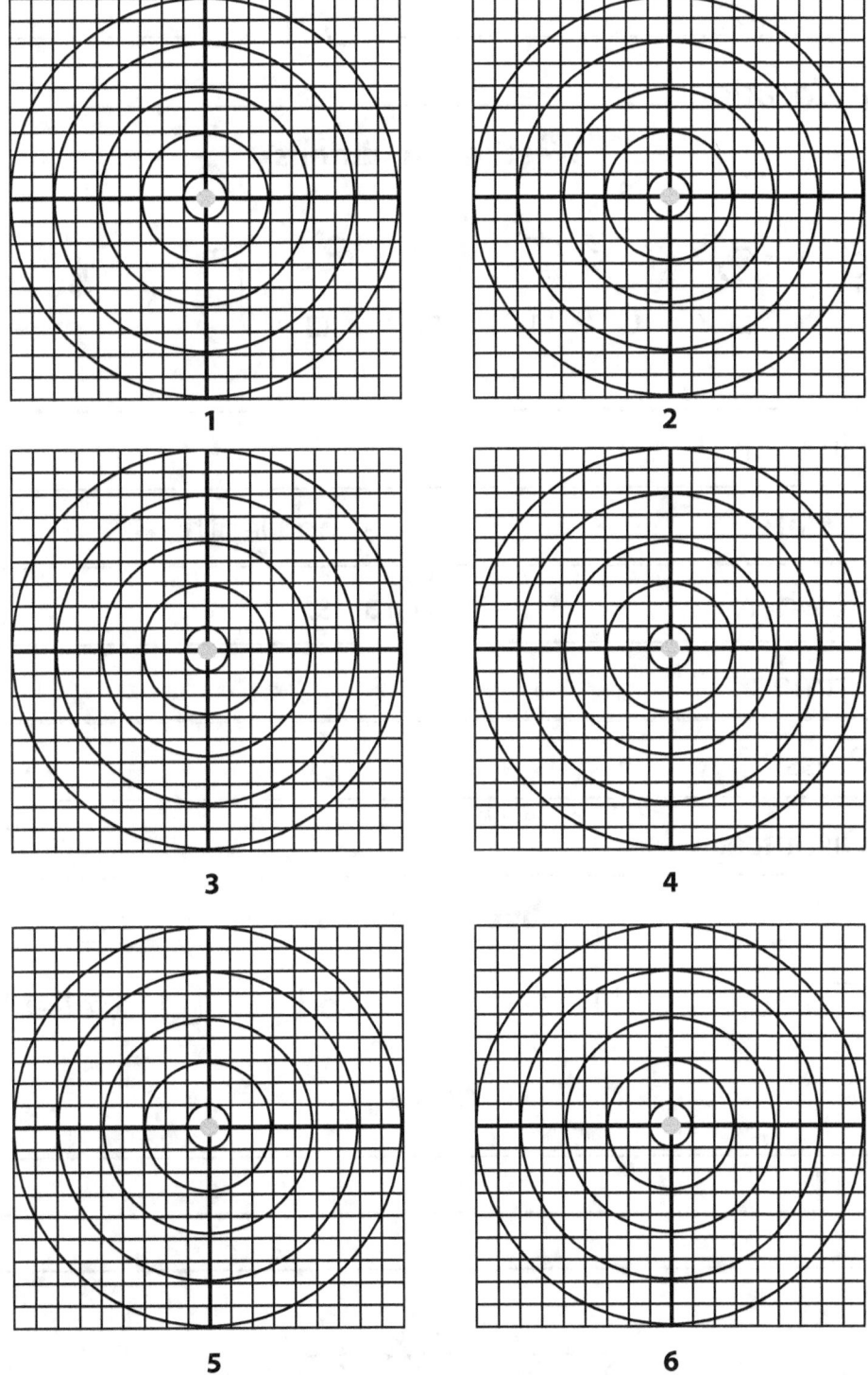

📅 Date: _____ 🕐 Time: _____

📍 Location: _____

Weather Conditions

☀️   ⛅   🌤️   🌧️   ☁️   🌨️   🚩 _____   🌡️ _____
☐   ☐   ☐   ☐   ☐   ☐

Firearm:	
Bullet:	Seating Depth:
Powder:	Grains:
Primer:	
Brass:	
Distance:	

Overall Results

☐ Poor   ☐ Fair   ☐ Good   ☐ Excellent

Notes

_____

_____

_____

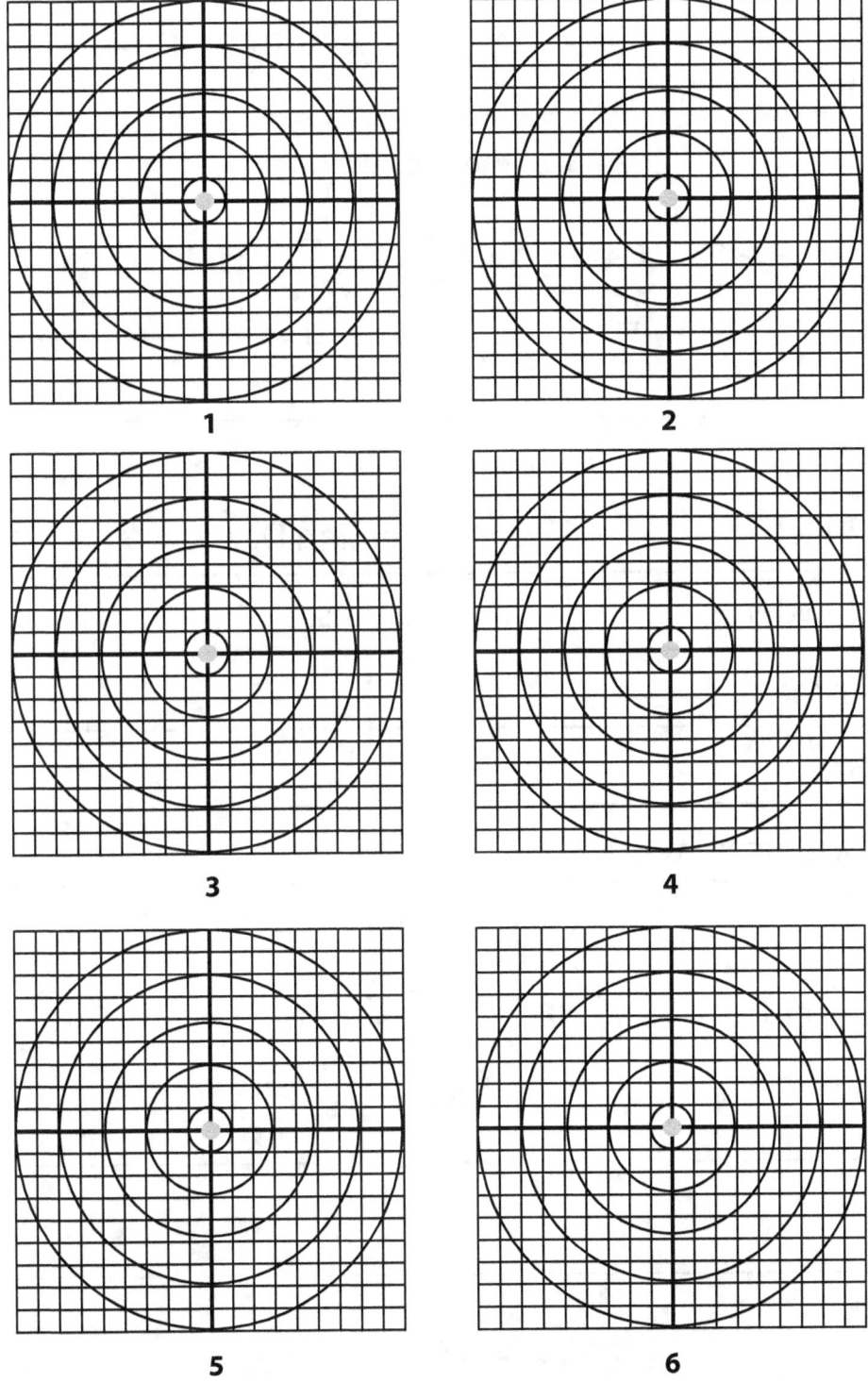

📅 Date: _____ 🕐 Time: _____

📍 Location: _____

Weather Conditions

☀️ ☐   ⛅ ☐   🌤 ☐   🌧 ☐   🌨 ☐   🌦 ☐   🚩 _____   🌡 _____

Firearm:	
Bullet:	Seating Depth:
Powder:	Grains:
Primer:	
Brass:	
Distance:	

Overall Results

☐ Poor   ☐ Fair   ☐ Good   ☐ Excellent

Notes

_____

_____

_____

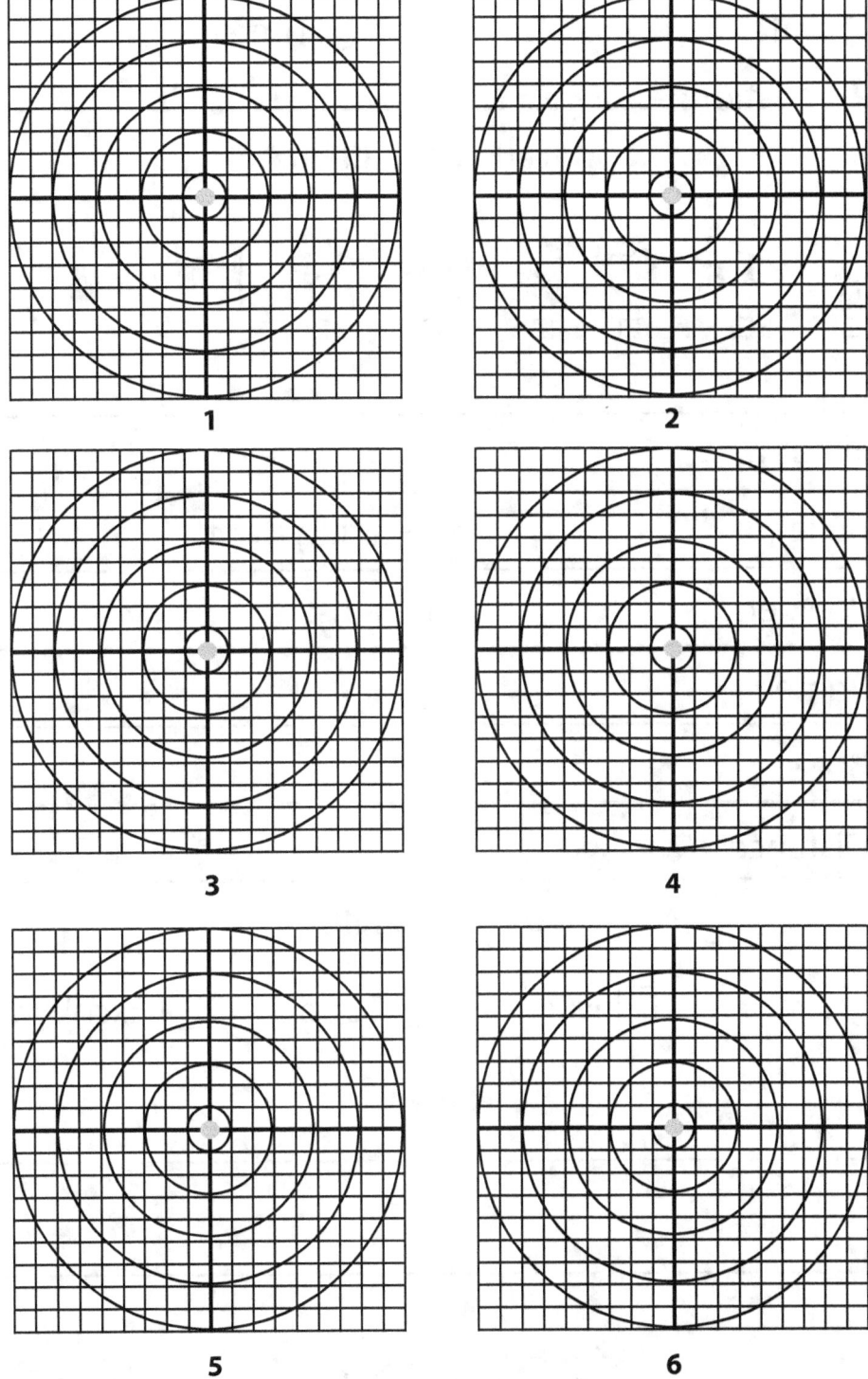

📅 Date: _____   🕐 Time: _____

📍 Location: _____

Weather Conditions

☀️ ☁️ 🌤️ ⛅ 🌧️ 🌨️ 🚩 🌡️
☐ ☐ ☐ ☐ ☐ ☐ ____ ____

Firearm:	
Bullet:	Seating Depth:
Powder:	Grains:
Primer:	
Brass:	
Distance:	

Overall Results

☐ Poor   ☐ Fair   ☐ Good   ☐ Excellent

Notes

_____

_____

☆ ☆ ☆ ☆ ☆

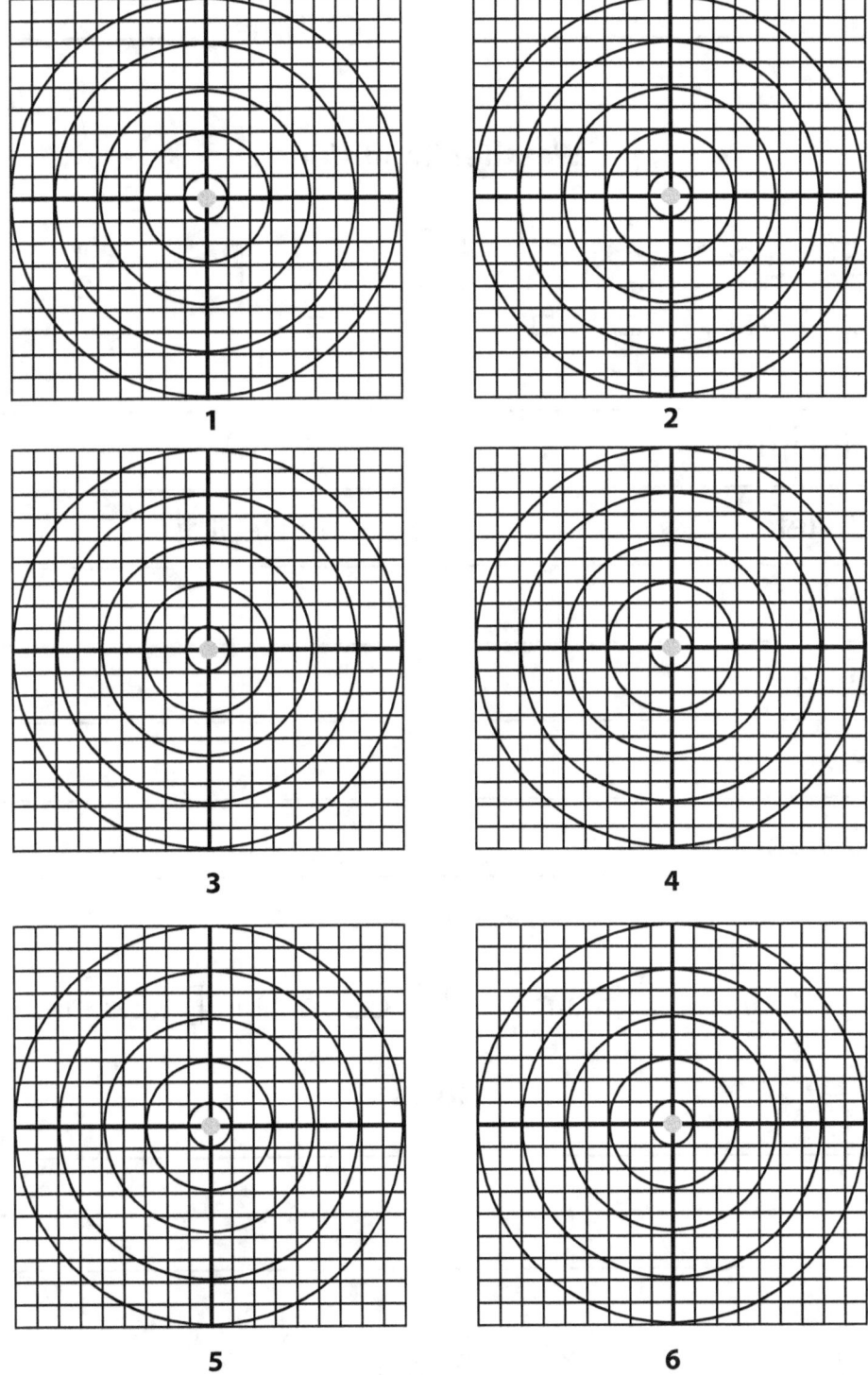

📅 Date: _____ 🕐 Time: _____

📍 Location: _____

Weather Conditions

☀️ ☁️ ⛅ 🌧️ 🌧️ 🌨️ 🚩 _____ 🌡️ _____
☐ ☐ ☐ ☐ ☐ ☐

Firearm:	
Bullet:	Seating Depth:
Powder:	Grains:
Primer:	
Brass:	
Distance:	

Overall Results

☐ Poor ☐ Fair ☐ Good ☐ Excellent

Notes

_____
_____
_____

☆ ☆ ☆ ☆ ☆

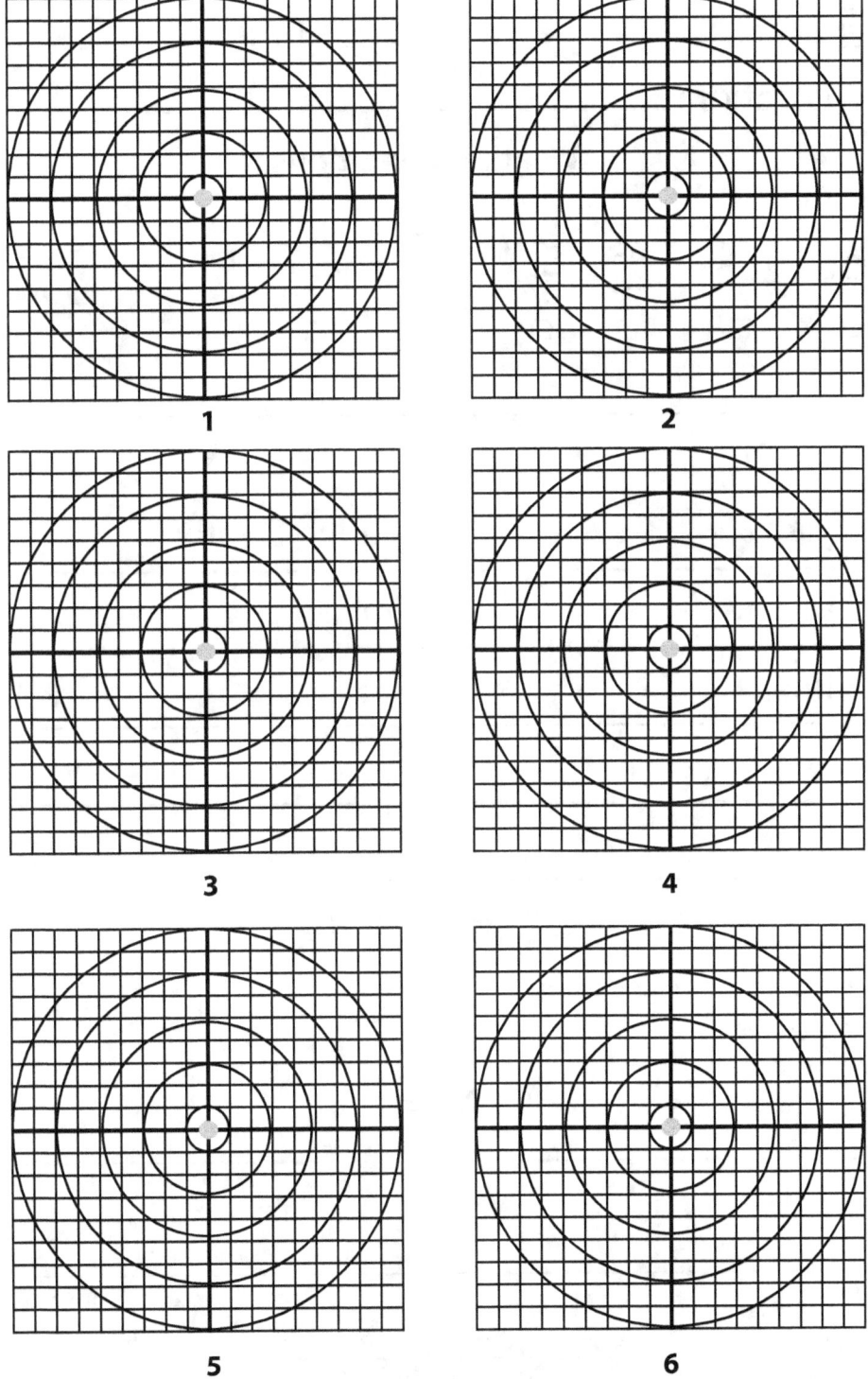

📅 Date: _____   🕐 Time: _____

📍 Location: _____

Weather Conditions

☀️ ☁️ ⛅ 🌦️ 🌧️ 🌨️ 🚩 _____ 🌡️ _____
☐   ☐   ☐   ☐   ☐   ☐

Firearm:	
Bullet:	Seating Depth:
Powder:	Grains:
Primer:	
Brass:	
Distance:	

Overall Results

☐ Poor   ☐ Fair   ☐ Good   ☐ Excellent

Notes

_____

_____

_____

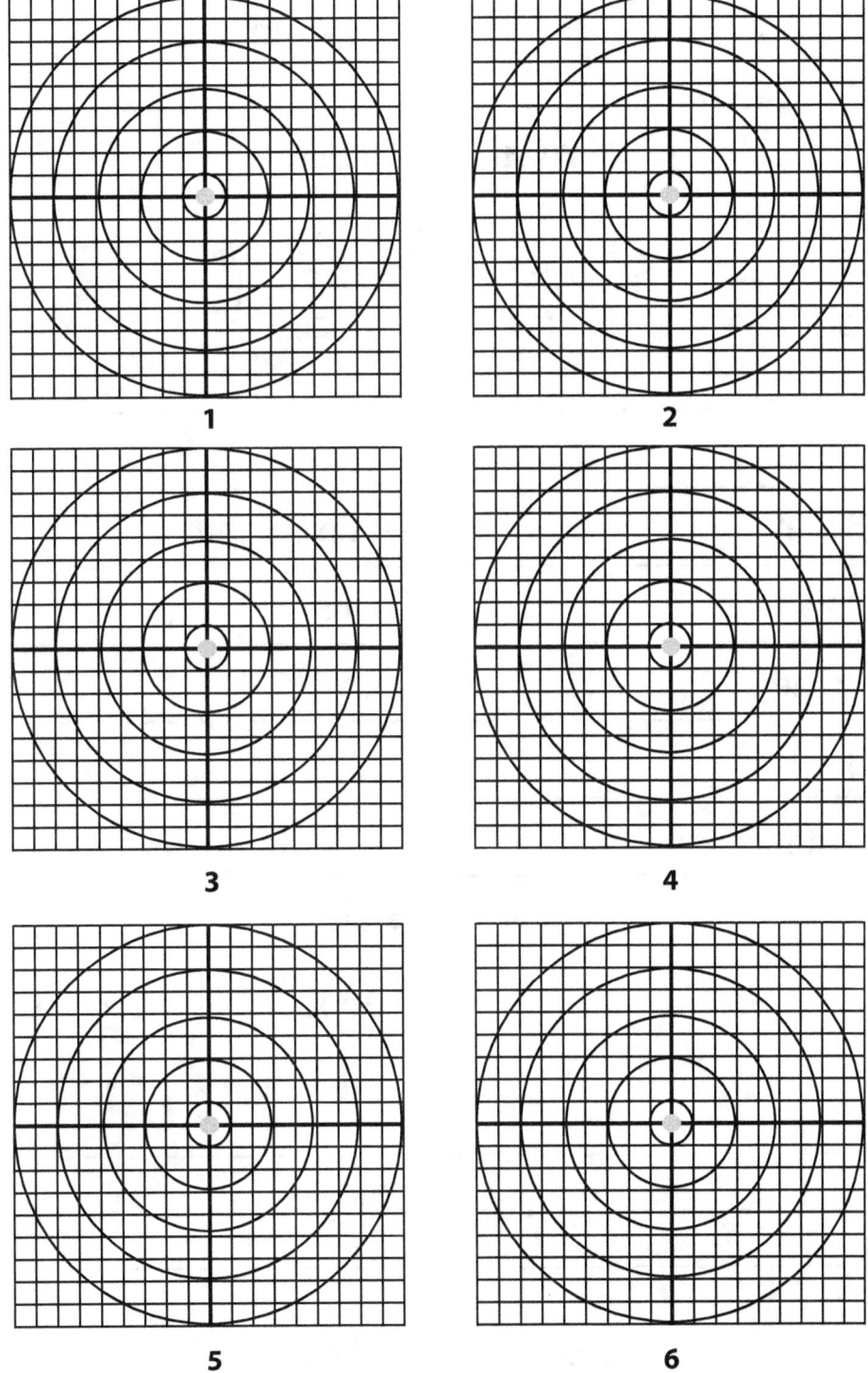

📅 Date: _____ 🕐 Time: _____

📍 Location: _____

Weather Conditions

☀️ ☁️ 🌤️ 🌧️ 🌧️ 🌨️ 🚩 _____ 🌡️ _____

☐ ☐ ☐ ☐ ☐ ☐

Firearm:	
Bullet:	Seating Depth:
Powder:	Grains:
Primer:	
Brass:	
Distance:	

Overall Results

☐ Poor   ☐ Fair   ☐ Good   ☐ Excellent

Notes

_____
_____
_____

☆ ☆ ☆ ☆ ☆

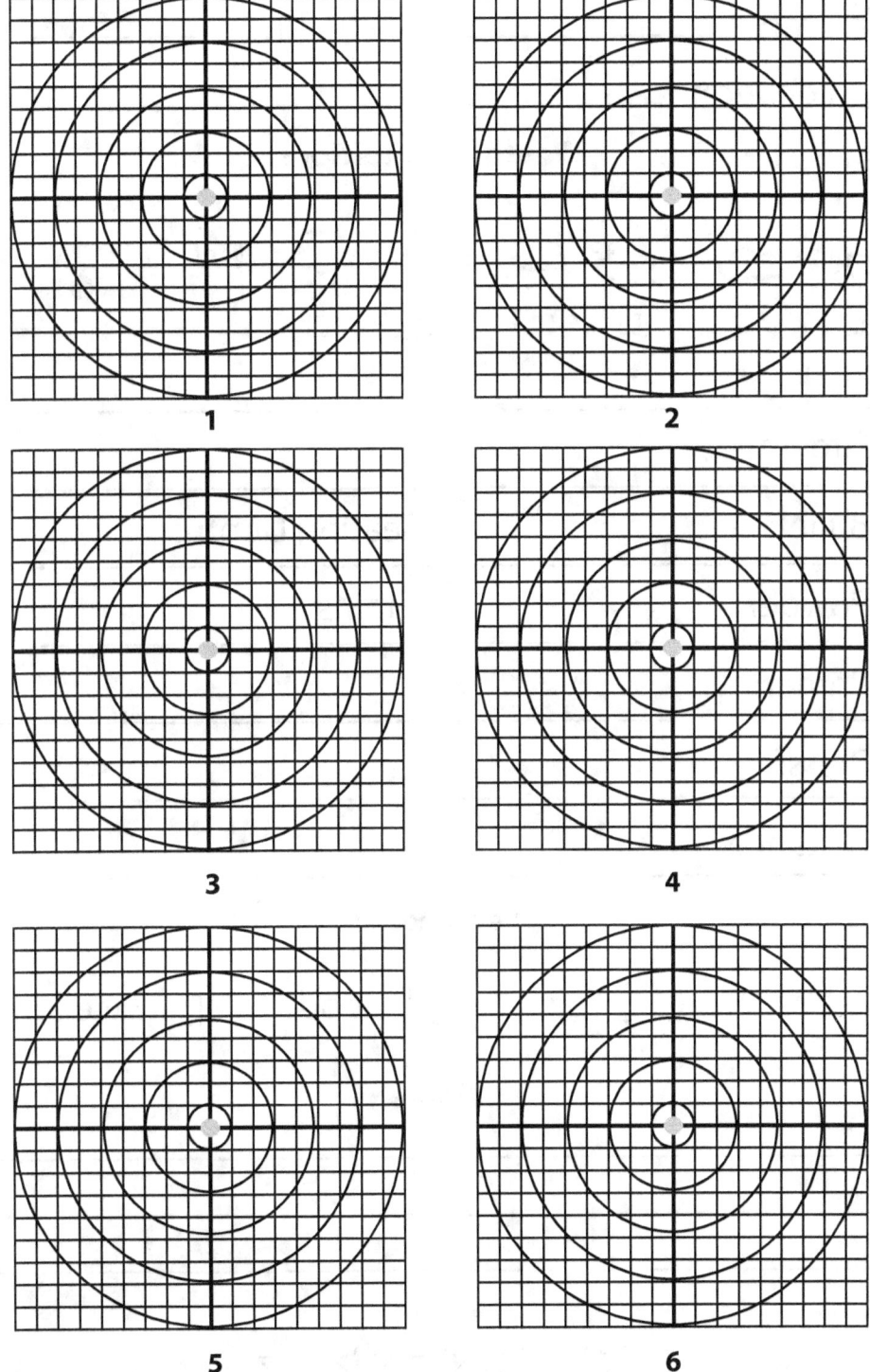

🗓 Date: _____ 🕐 Time: _____

📍 Location: _____

Weather Conditions

☀ ☁ ⛅ ☁ 🌧 🌨 🚩 _____ 🌡 _____
☐ ☐ ☐ ☐ ☐ ☐

Firearm:	
Bullet:	Seating Depth:
Powder:	Grains:
Primer:	
Brass:	
Distance:	

Overall Results

☐ Poor ☐ Fair ☐ Good ☐ Excellent

Notes

_____
_____
_____

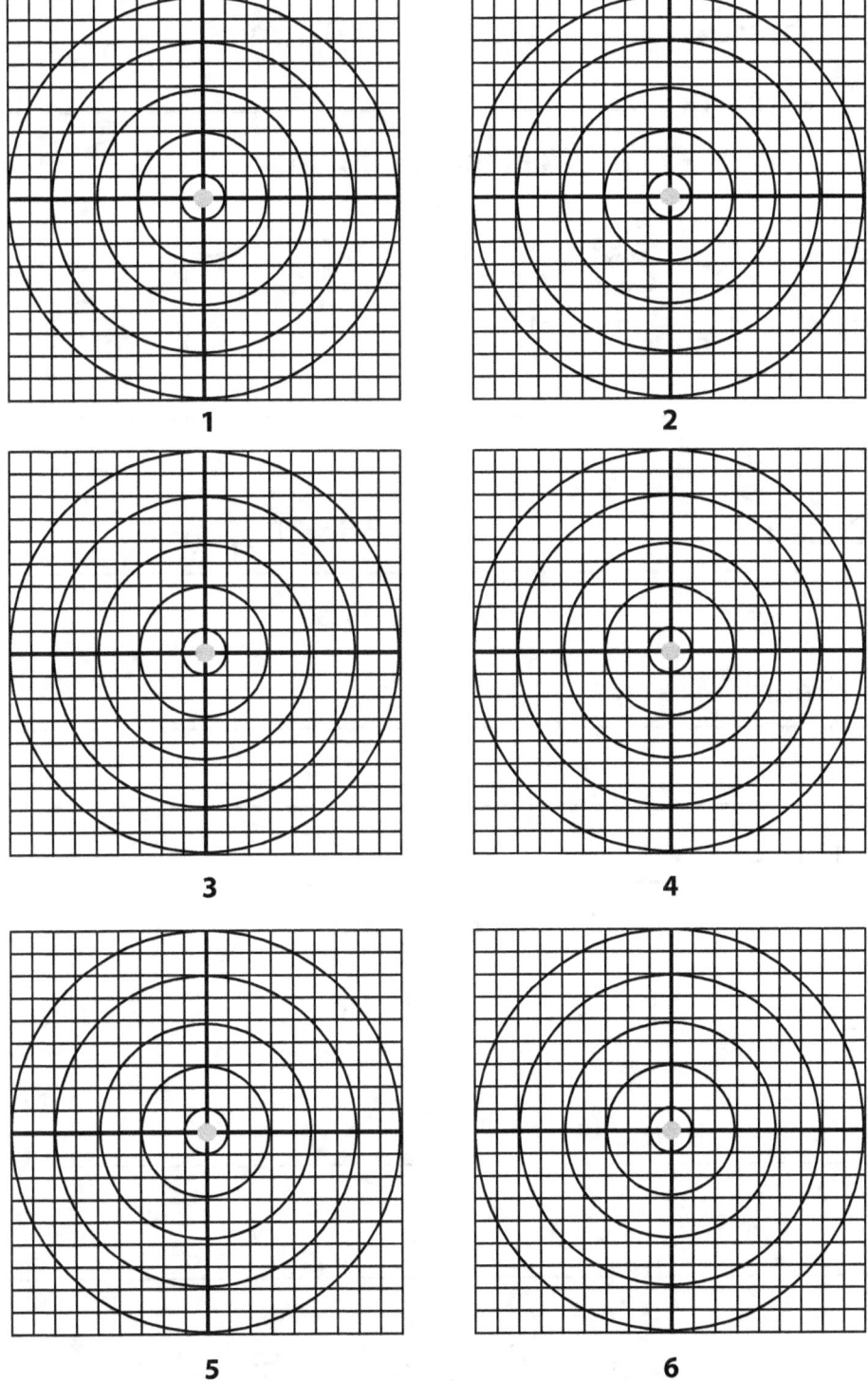

Date: _____ Time: _____

Location: _____

Weather Conditions

☀ ☁ ⛅ 🌦 🌧 🌨 🚩_____ 🌡_____
☐ ☐ ☐ ☐ ☐ ☐

Firearm:	
Bullet:	Seating Depth:
Powder:	Grains:
Primer:	
Brass:	
Distance:	

Overall Results

☐ Poor   ☐ Fair   ☐ Good   ☐ Excellent

Notes

_____
_____
_____

☆ ☆ ☆ ☆ ☆

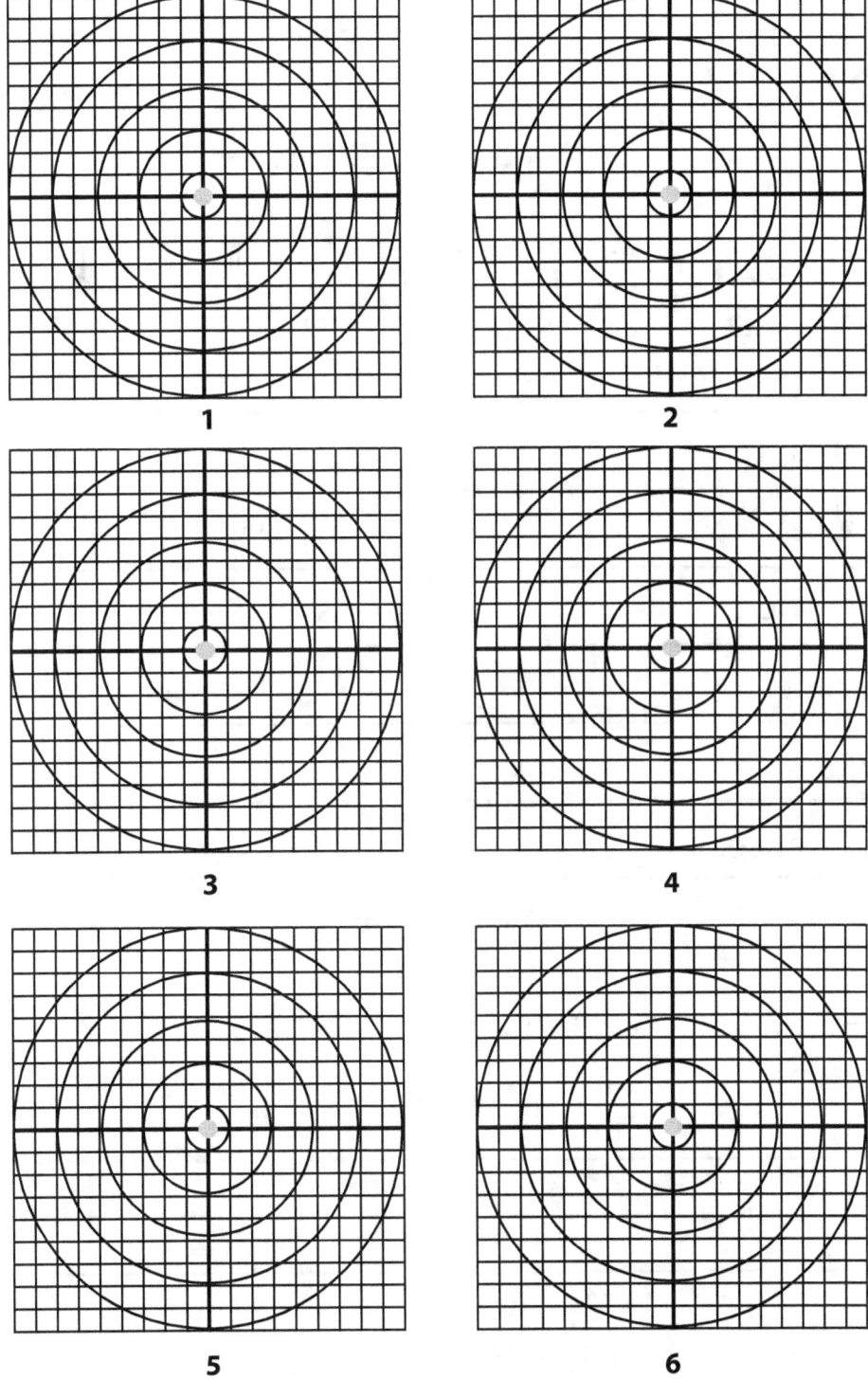

Date: _____ Time: _____

Location: _____

Weather Conditions

☀ ☐ ⛅ ☐ 🌤 ☐ ☁ ☐ 🌧 ☐ 🌨 ☐ 🚩 _____ 🌡 _____

Firearm:	
Bullet:	Seating Depth:
Powder:	Grains:
Primer:	
Brass:	
Distance:	

Overall Results

☐ Poor   ☐ Fair   ☐ Good   ☐ Excellent

Notes

_____
_____
_____

☆ ☆ ☆ ☆ ☆

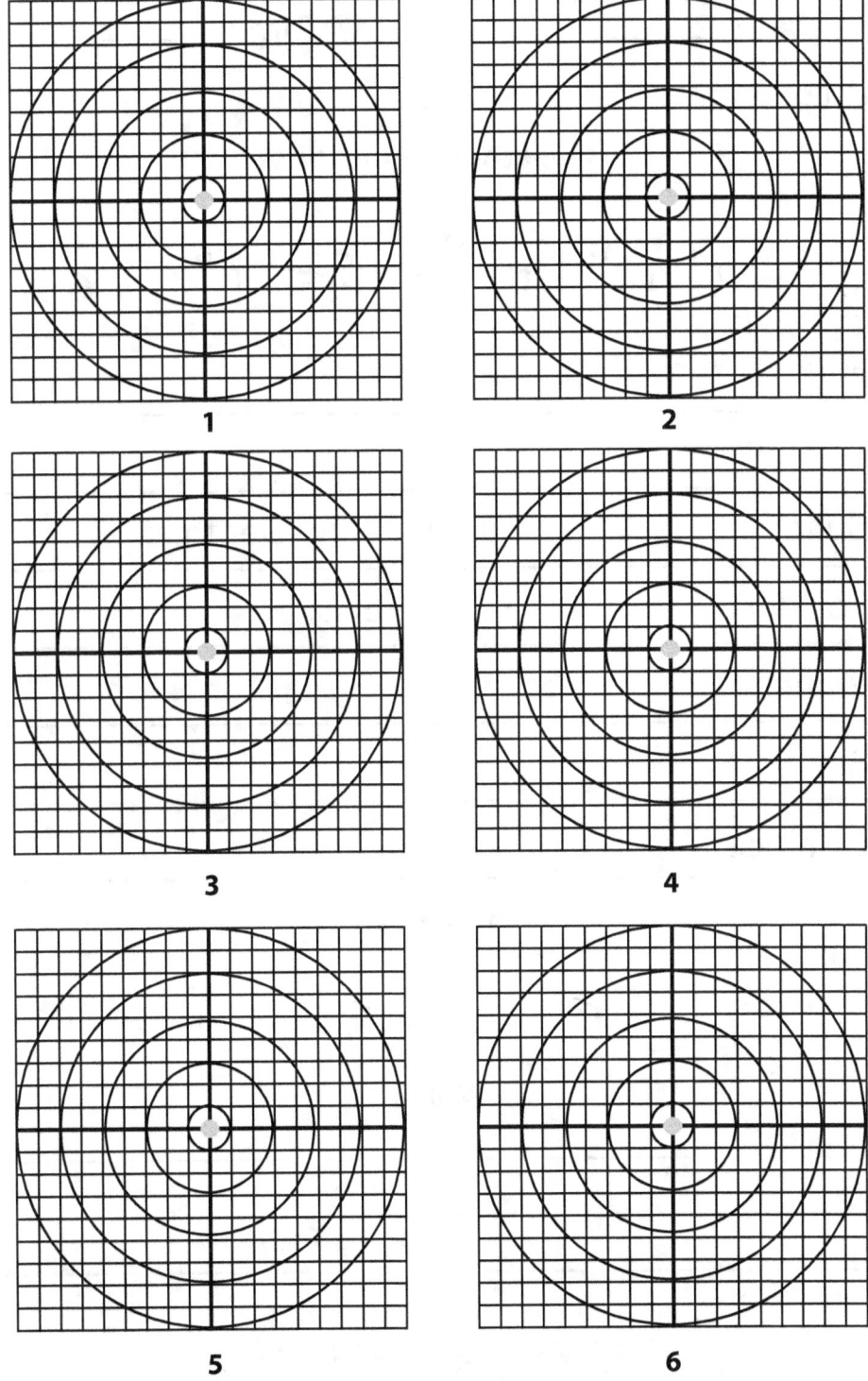

📅 Date: _____ 🕐 Time: _____

📍 Location: _____

Weather Conditions

☀️ ☁️ ⛅ 🌧️ 🌧️ 🌨️ 🚩 _____ 🌡️ _____
☐   ☐   ☐   ☐   ☐   ☐

Firearm:	
Bullet:	Seating Depth:
Powder:	Grains:
Primer:	
Brass:	
Distance:	

Overall Results

☐ Poor   ☐ Fair   ☐ Good   ☐ Excellent

Notes

_____
_____
_____

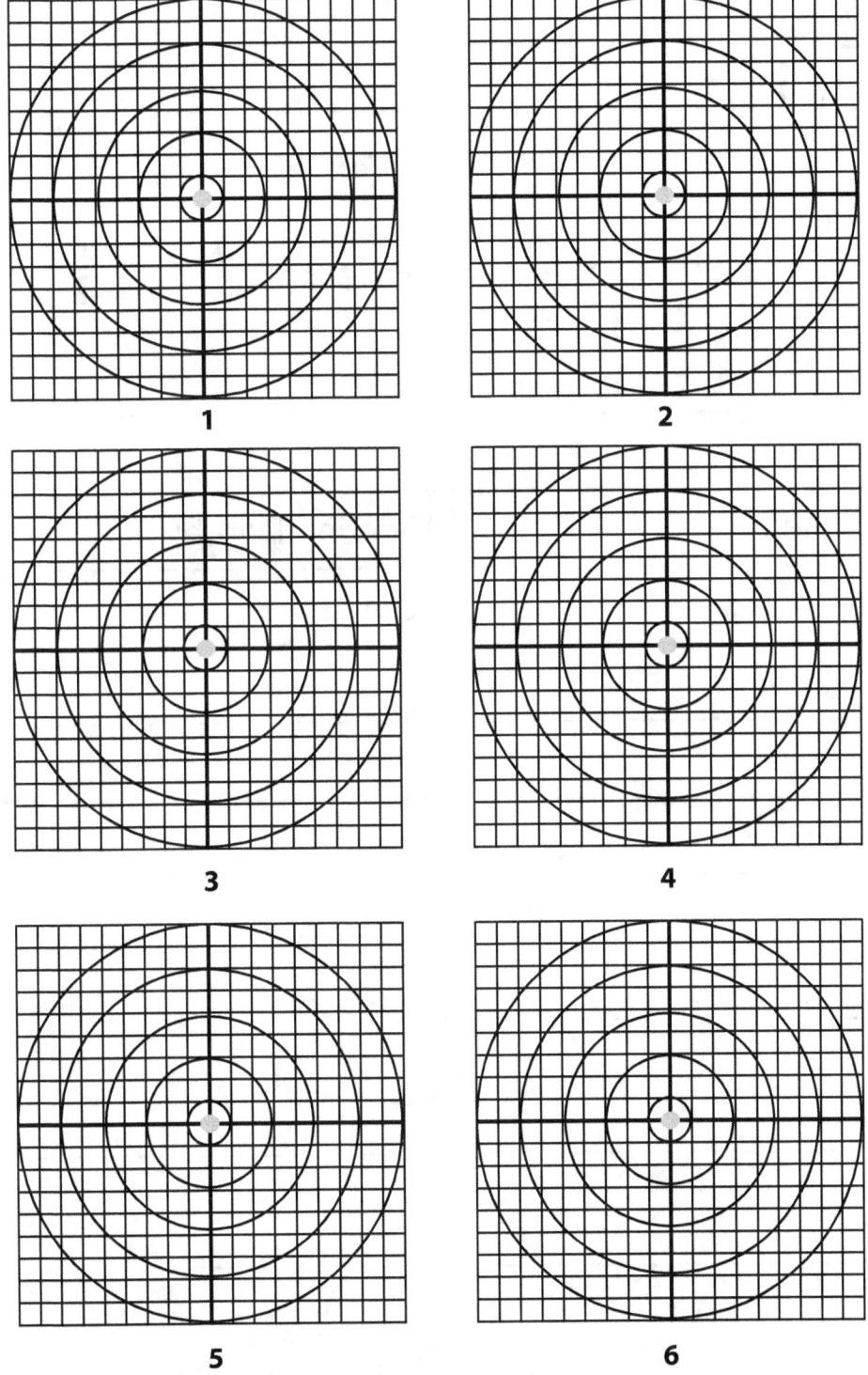

Date: _____ Time: _____

Location: _____

Weather Conditions

☀ ☁ ⛅ 🌥 🌧 🌨 🚩 🌡

☐ ☐ ☐ ☐ ☐ ☐ _____ _____

Firearm:	
Bullet:	Seating Depth:
Powder:	Grains:
Primer:	
Brass:	
Distance:	

Overall Results

☐ Poor   ☐ Fair   ☐ Good   ☐ Excellent

Notes

_____
_____
_____

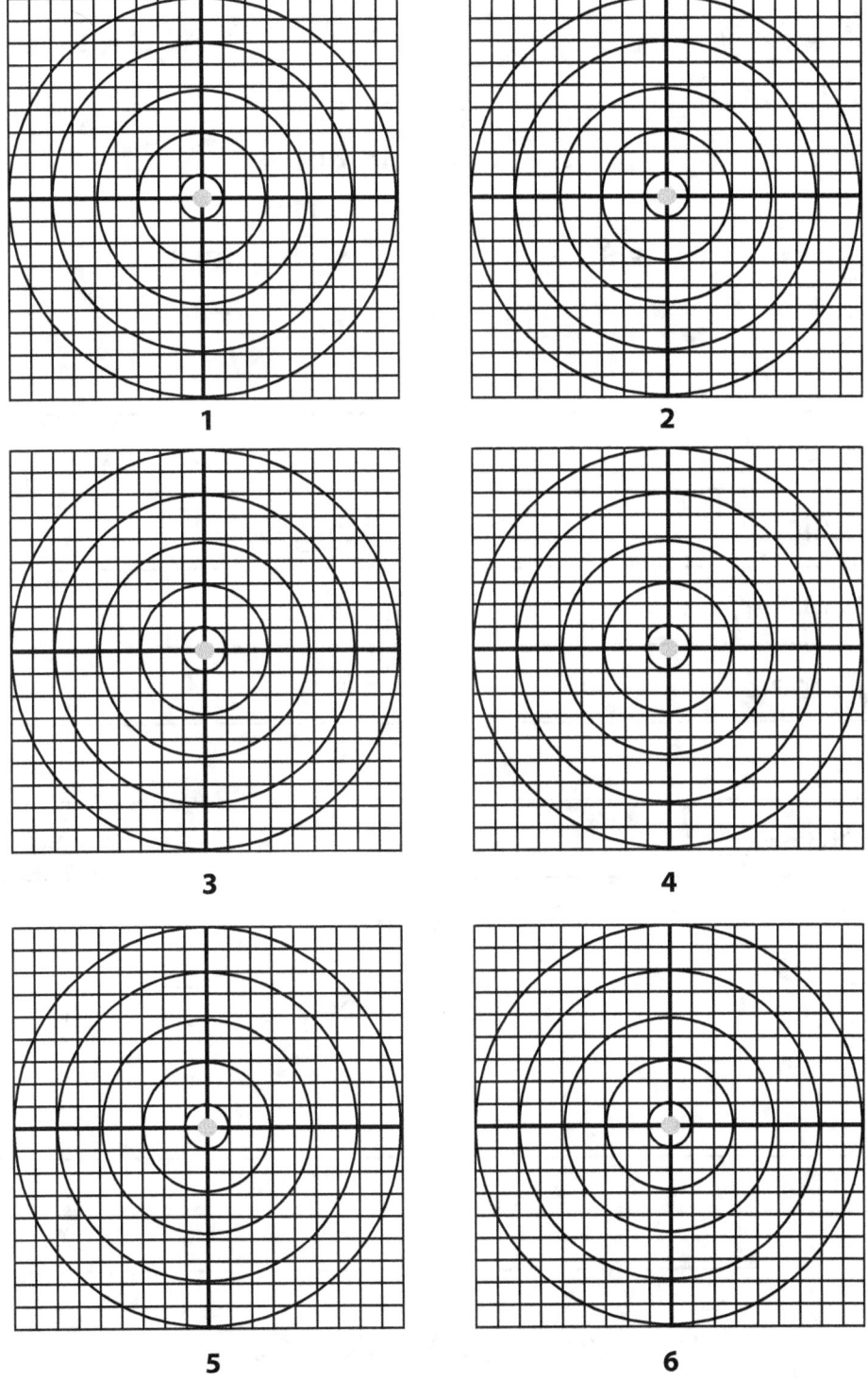

Date: _____   Time: _____

 Location: _____

Weather Conditions

☀ ☁ ⛅ ☁ 🌧 🌨 🚩 🌡
☐ ☐ ☐ ☐ ☐ ☐ _____ _____

Firearm:	
Bullet:	Seating Depth:
Powder:	Grains:
Primer:	
Brass:	
Distance:	

Overall Results

☐ Poor   ☐ Fair   ☐ Good   ☐ Excellent

Notes

_____
_____
_____

☆ ☆ ☆ ☆ ☆

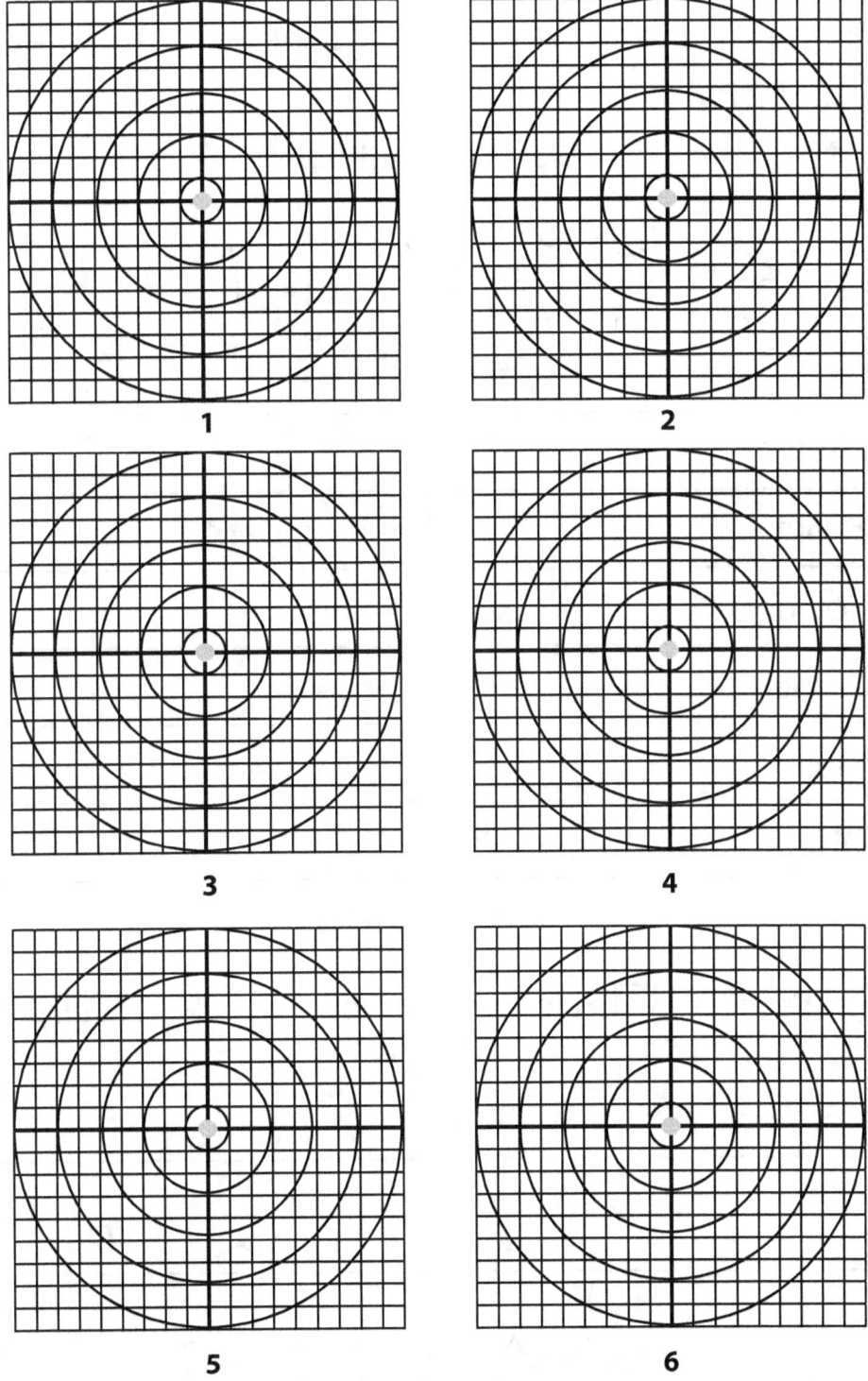

📅 Date: _____   🕐 Time: _____

📍 Location: _____

Weather Conditions

☀️ ☁️ ⛅ 🌧️ 🌧️ 🌨️ 🚩 🌡️
☐ ☐ ☐ ☐ ☐ ☐ ___ ___

Firearm:	
Bullet:	Seating Depth:
Powder:	Grains:
Primer:	
Brass:	
Distance:	

Overall Results

☐ Poor   ☐ Fair   ☐ Good   ☐ Excellent

Notes

_____
_____
_____

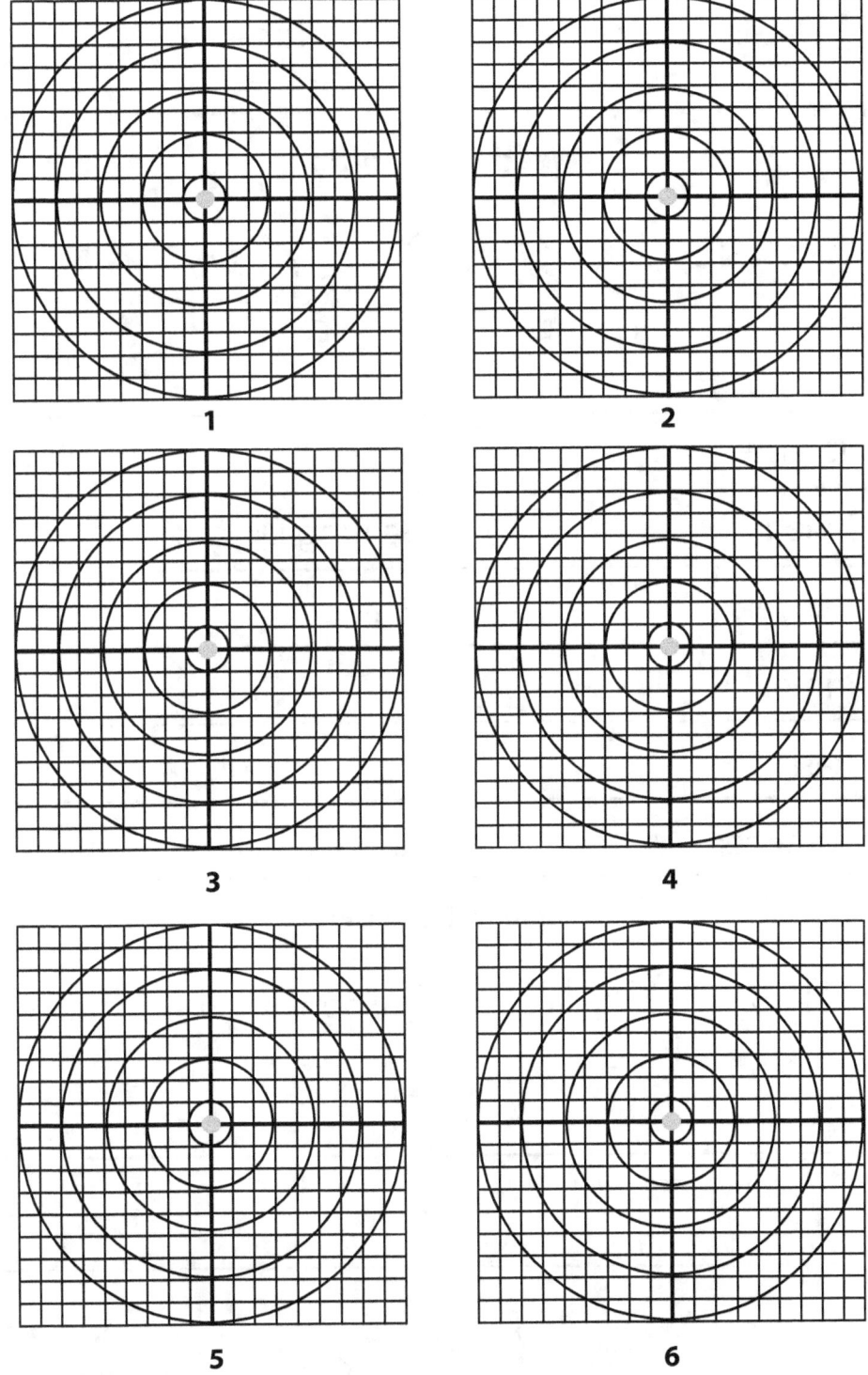

📅 Date: _____ 🕐 Time: _____

📍 Location: _____

Weather Conditions

☀️ ☁️ ⛅ 🌧️ 🌧️ 🌨️ 🚩 🌡️
☐   ☐   ☐   ☐   ☐   ☐   _____ _____

Firearm:	
Bullet:	Seating Depth:
Powder:	Grains:
Primer:	
Brass:	
Distance:	

Overall Results

☐ Poor   ☐ Fair   ☐ Good   ☐ Excellent

Notes

_____

_____

_____

☆ ☆ ☆ ☆ ☆

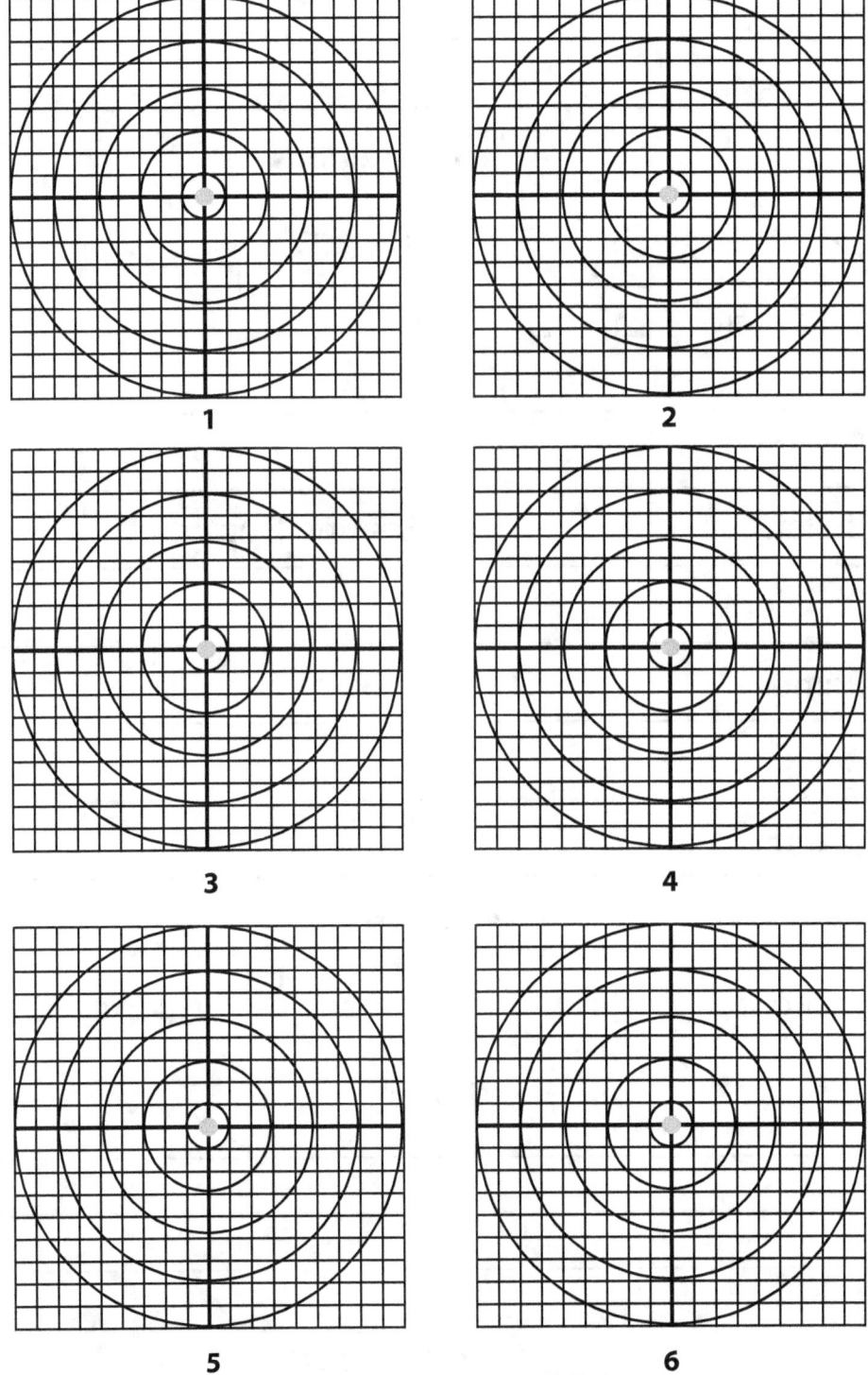

Date: _____ Time: _____

Location: _____

Weather Conditions

☐ ☐ ☐ ☐ ☐ ☐ ☐ _____ 🌡 _____

Firearm:	
Bullet:	Seating Depth:
Powder:	Grains:
Primer:	
Brass:	
Distance:	

Overall Results

☐ Poor ☐ Fair ☐ Good ☐ Excellent

Notes

_____

_____

_____

☆ ☆ ☆ ☆ ☆

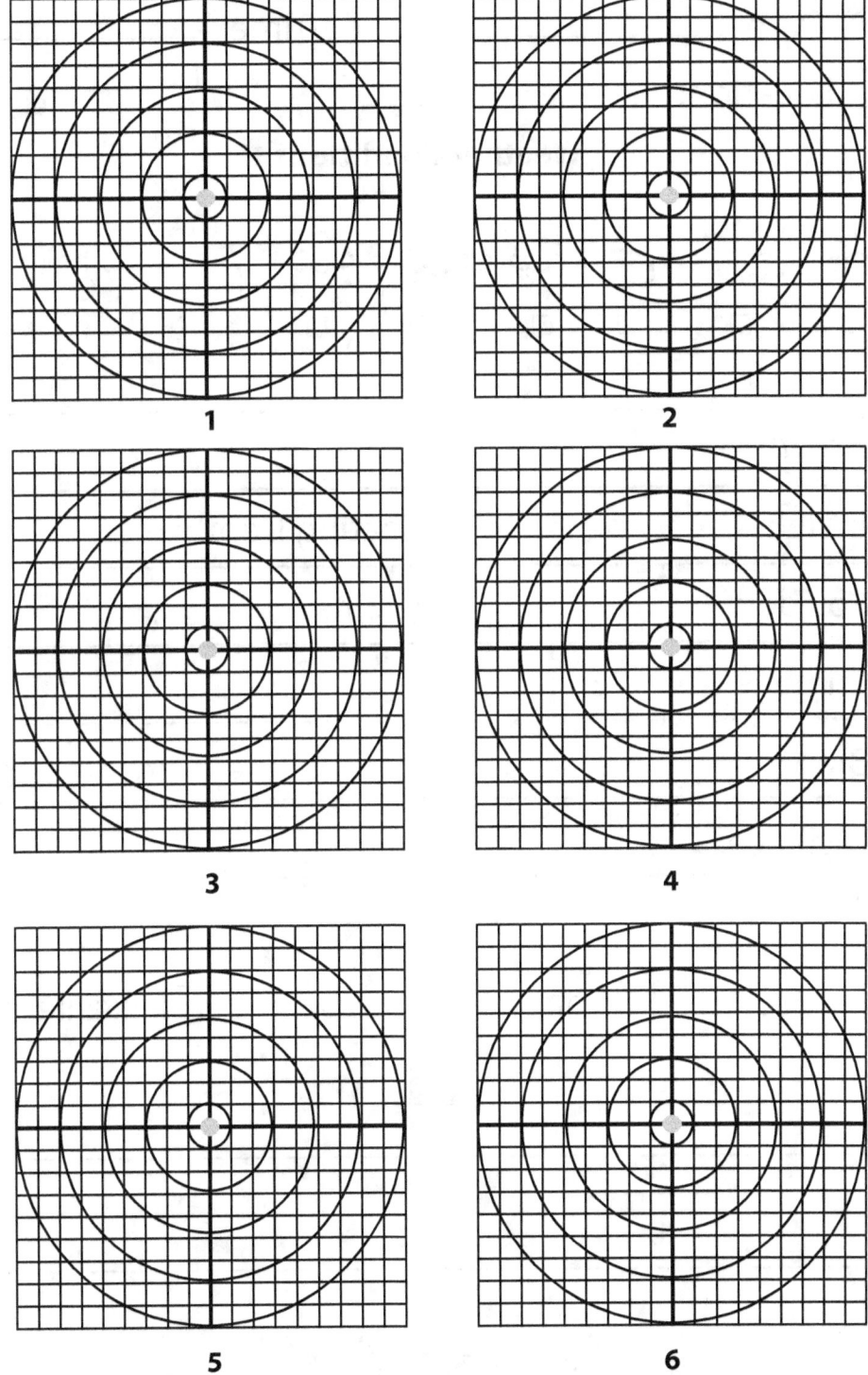

Date: _____ Time: _____

Location: _____

Weather Conditions

☀ ☁ ⛅ 🌧 🌧 🌨 🚩 🌡
☐ ☐ ☐ ☐ ☐ ☐ _____ _____

Firearm:	
Bullet:	Seating Depth:
Powder:	Grains:
Primer:	
Brass:	
Distance:	

Overall Results

☐ Poor   ☐ Fair   ☐ Good   ☐ Excellent

Notes

_____
_____

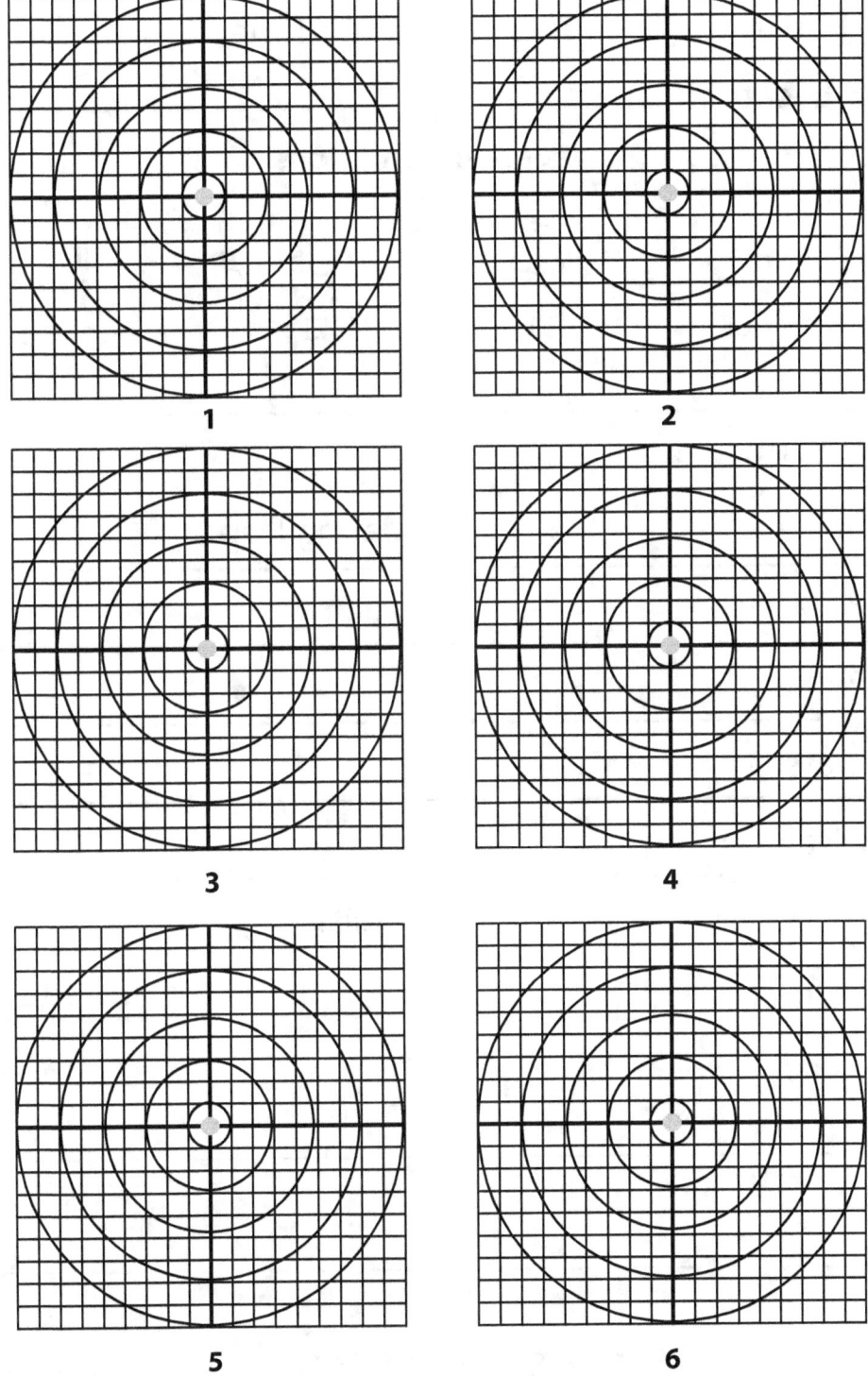

Date: _____ Time: _____

Location: _____

Weather Conditions

☀ ☁ ⛅ 🌦 🌧 🌨 🚩 _____ 🌡 _____

☐ ☐ ☐ ☐ ☐ ☐

Firearm:	
Bullet:	Seating Depth:
Powder:	Grains:
Primer:	
Brass:	
Distance:	

Overall Results

☐ Poor ☐ Fair ☐ Good ☐ Excellent

Notes

_____
_____
_____

☆ ☆ ☆ ☆ ☆

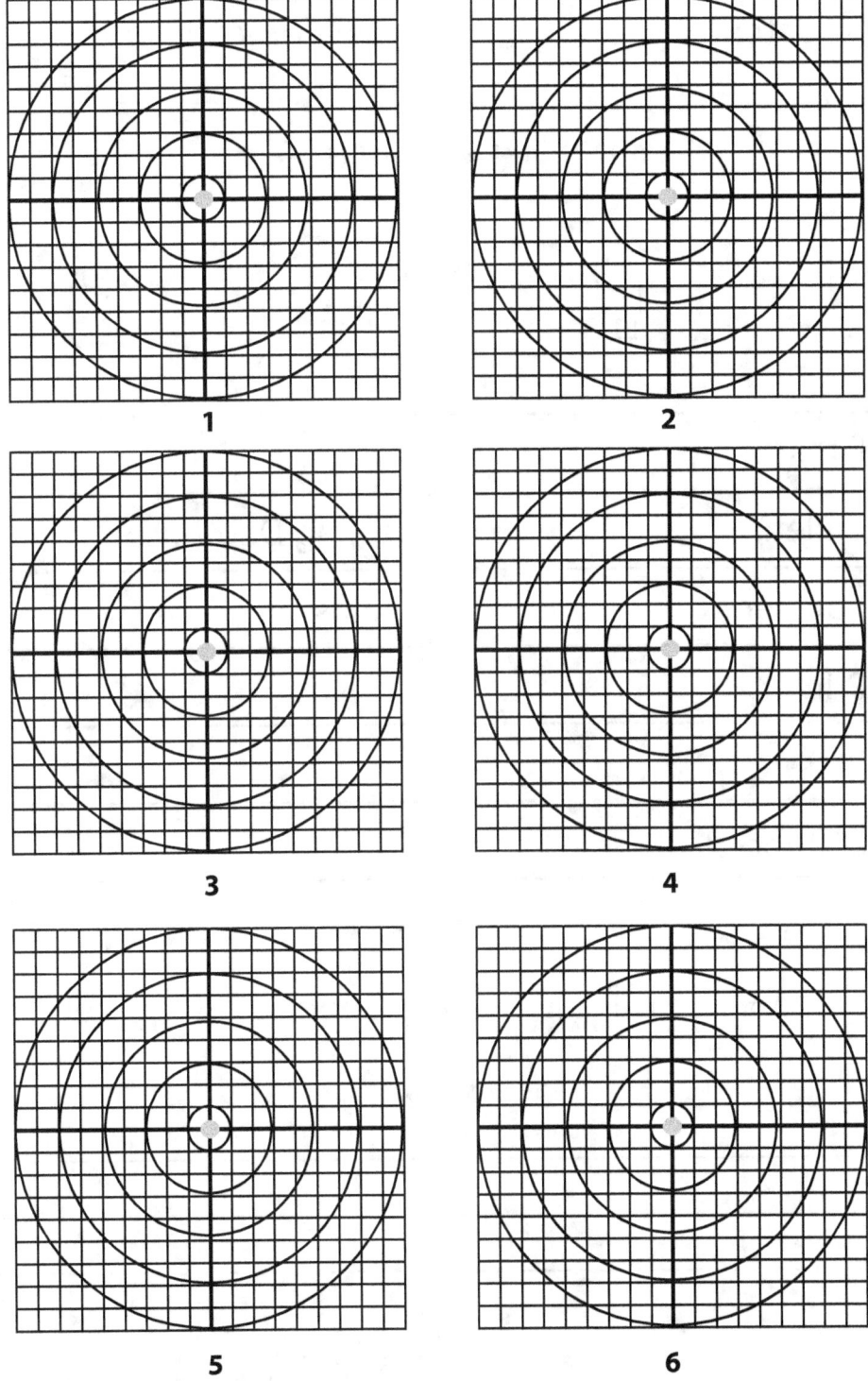

📅 Date: _____ 🕐 Time: _____

📍 Location: _____

Weather Conditions

☀ ☁ 🌤 ☁ 🌧 🌨 🚩 🌡
☐   ☐   ☐   ☐   ☐   ☐   ___ ___

Firearm:	
Bullet:	Seating Depth:
Powder:	Grains:
Primer:	
Brass:	
Distance:	

Overall Results

☐ Poor   ☐ Fair   ☐ Good   ☐ Excellent

Notes

_____
_____
_____

☆ ☆ ☆ ☆ ☆

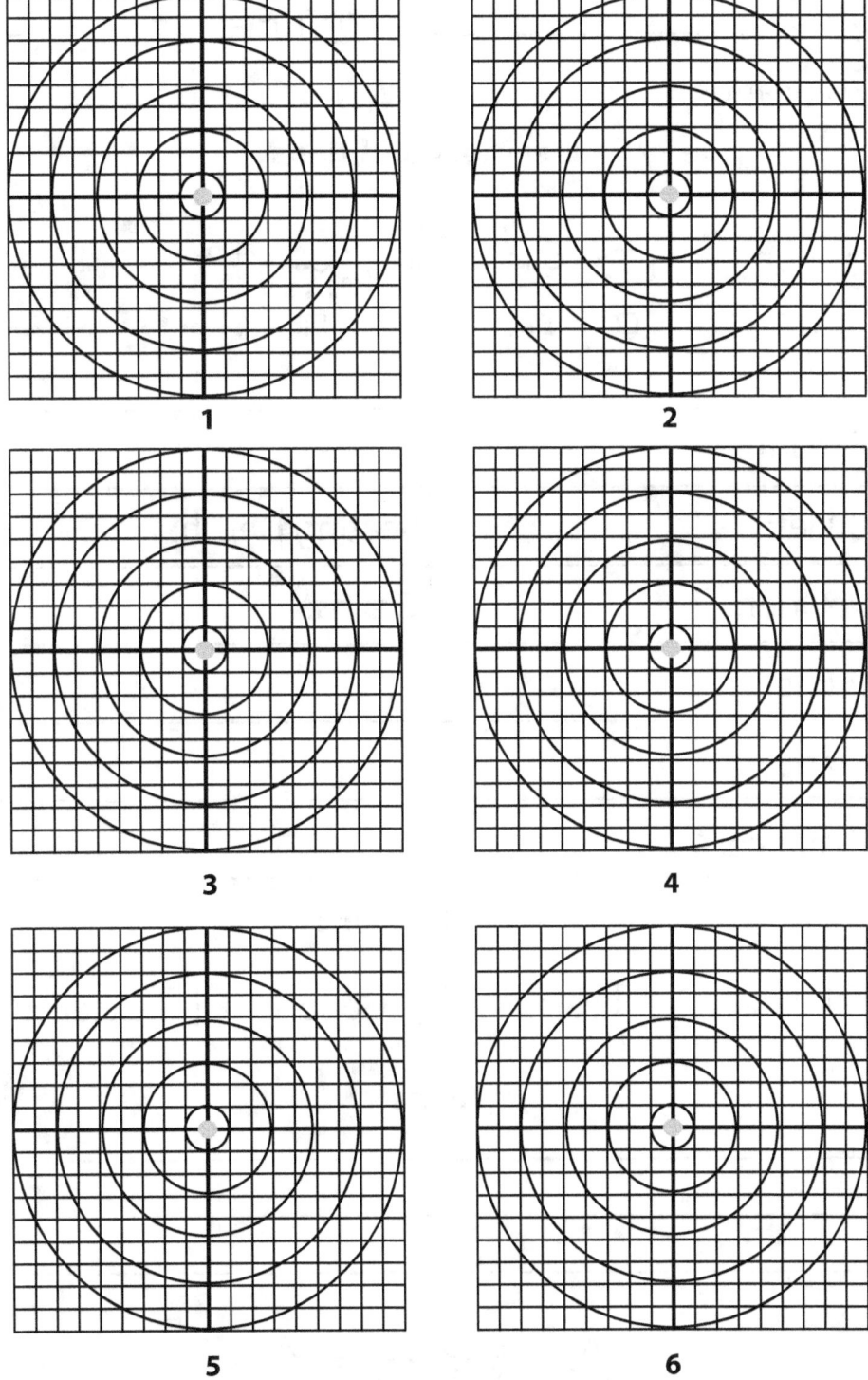

📅 Date: _____ 🕐 Time: _____

📍 Location: _____

Weather Conditions

☀️ ☁️ 🌤️ 🌧️ ⛈️ 🌨️ 🚩 _____ 🌡️ _____
☐   ☐   ☐   ☐   ☐   ☐

Firearm:	
Bullet:	Seating Depth:
Powder:	Grains:
Primer:	
Brass:	
Distance:	

Overall Results

☐ Poor ☐ Fair ☐ Good ☐ Excellent

Notes

_____
_____
_____

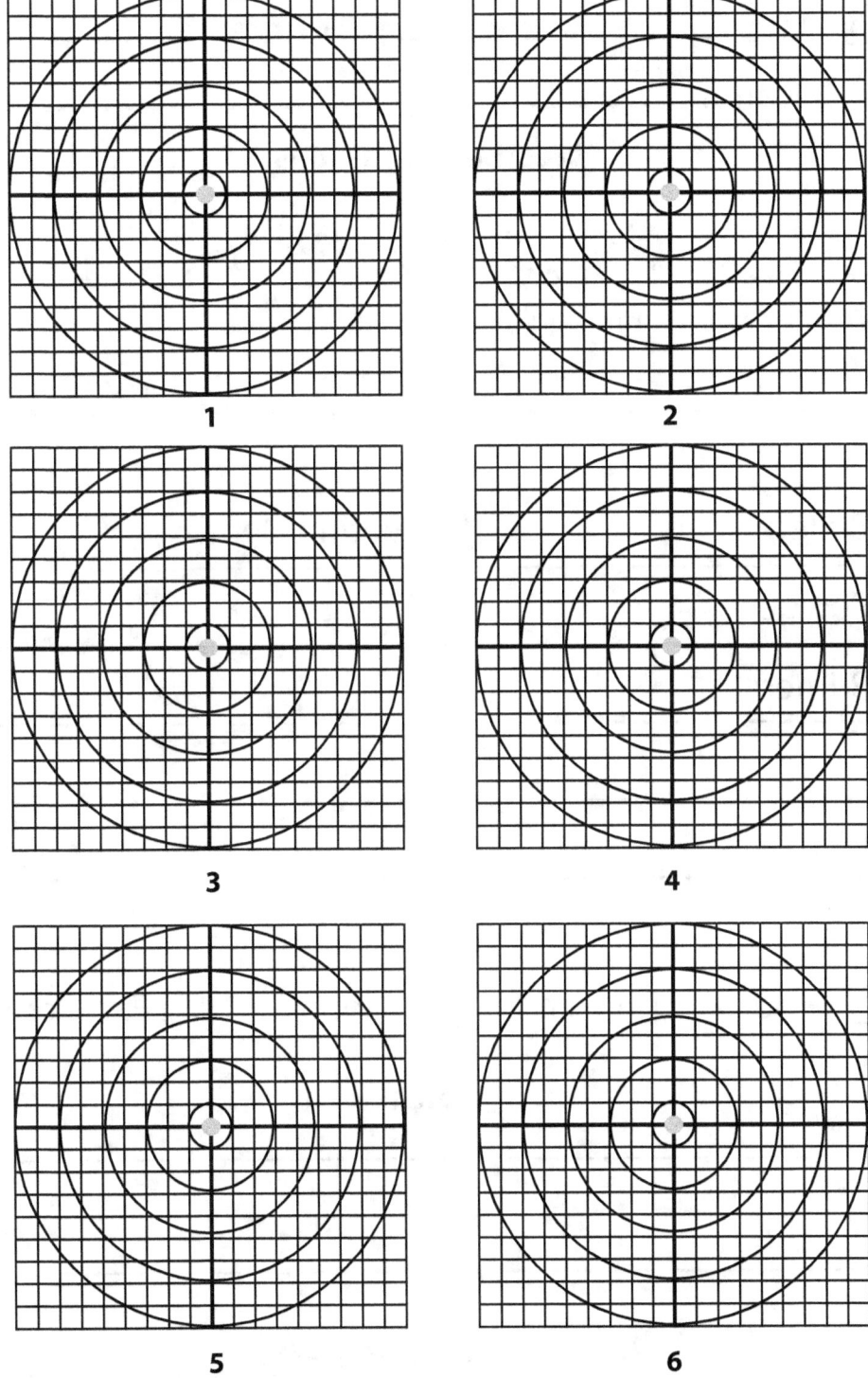

📅 Date: _____ 🕐 Time: _____

📍 Location: _____

Weather Conditions

☀️ ☁️ ⛅ 🌦️ 🌧️ 🌨️ 🚩 🌡️ _____
☐ ☐ ☐ ☐ ☐ ☐

Firearm:	
Bullet:	Seating Depth:
Powder:	Grains:
Primer:	
Brass:	
Distance:	

Overall Results

☐ Poor ☐ Fair ☐ Good ☐ Excellent

Notes

_____
_____
_____

☆ ☆ ☆ ☆ ☆

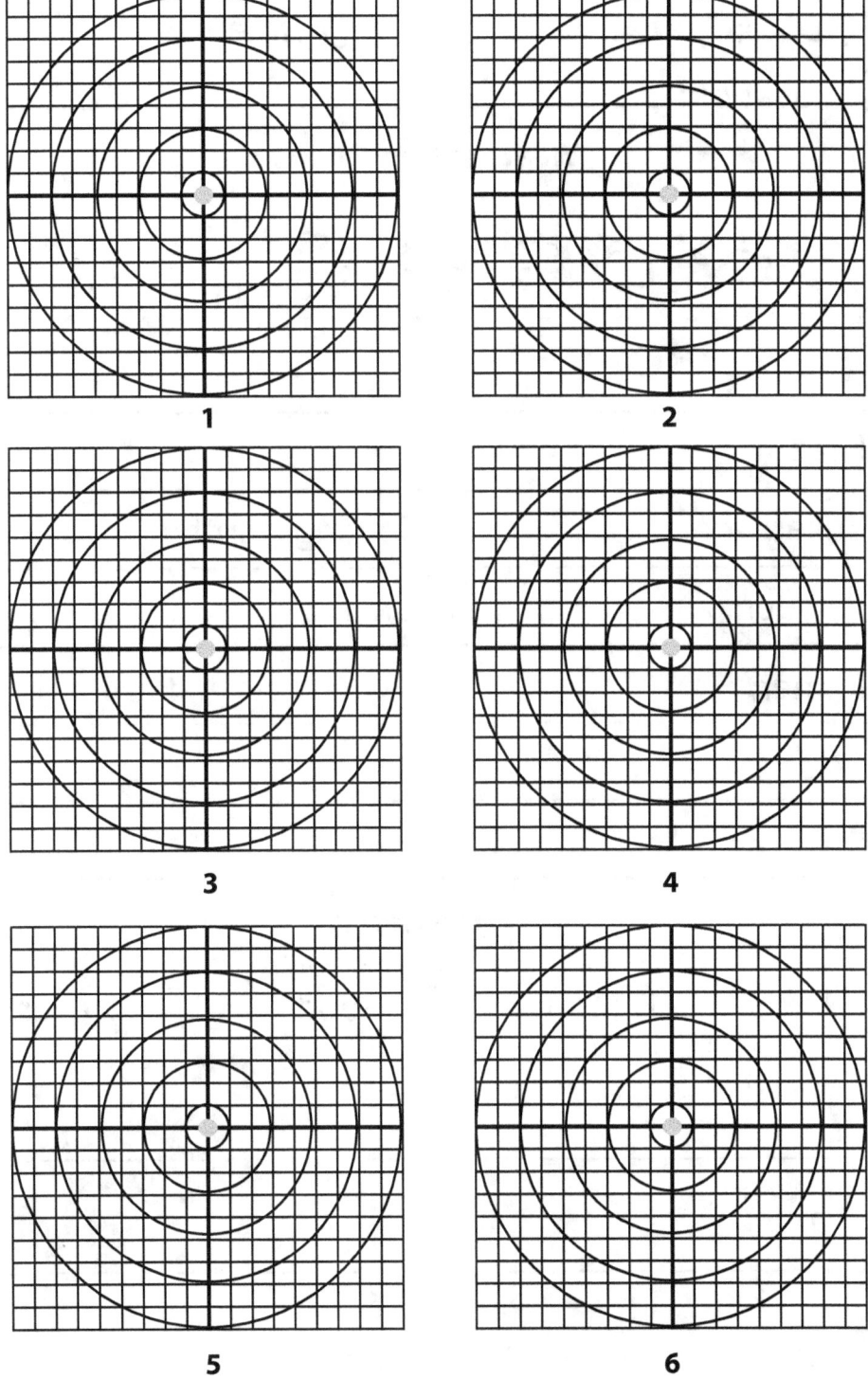

Date: _____ Time: _____
 Location: _____

Weather Conditions

☀ ☁ ⛅ 🌦 🌧 🌨 🚩 ____ 🌡 ____
☐   ☐   ☐   ☐   ☐   ☐

Firearm:	
Bullet:	Seating Depth:
Powder:	Grains:
Primer:	
Brass:	
Distance:	

Overall Results

☐ Poor ☐ Fair ☐ Good ☐ Excellent

Notes

_____
_____
_____

☆ ☆ ☆ ☆ ☆

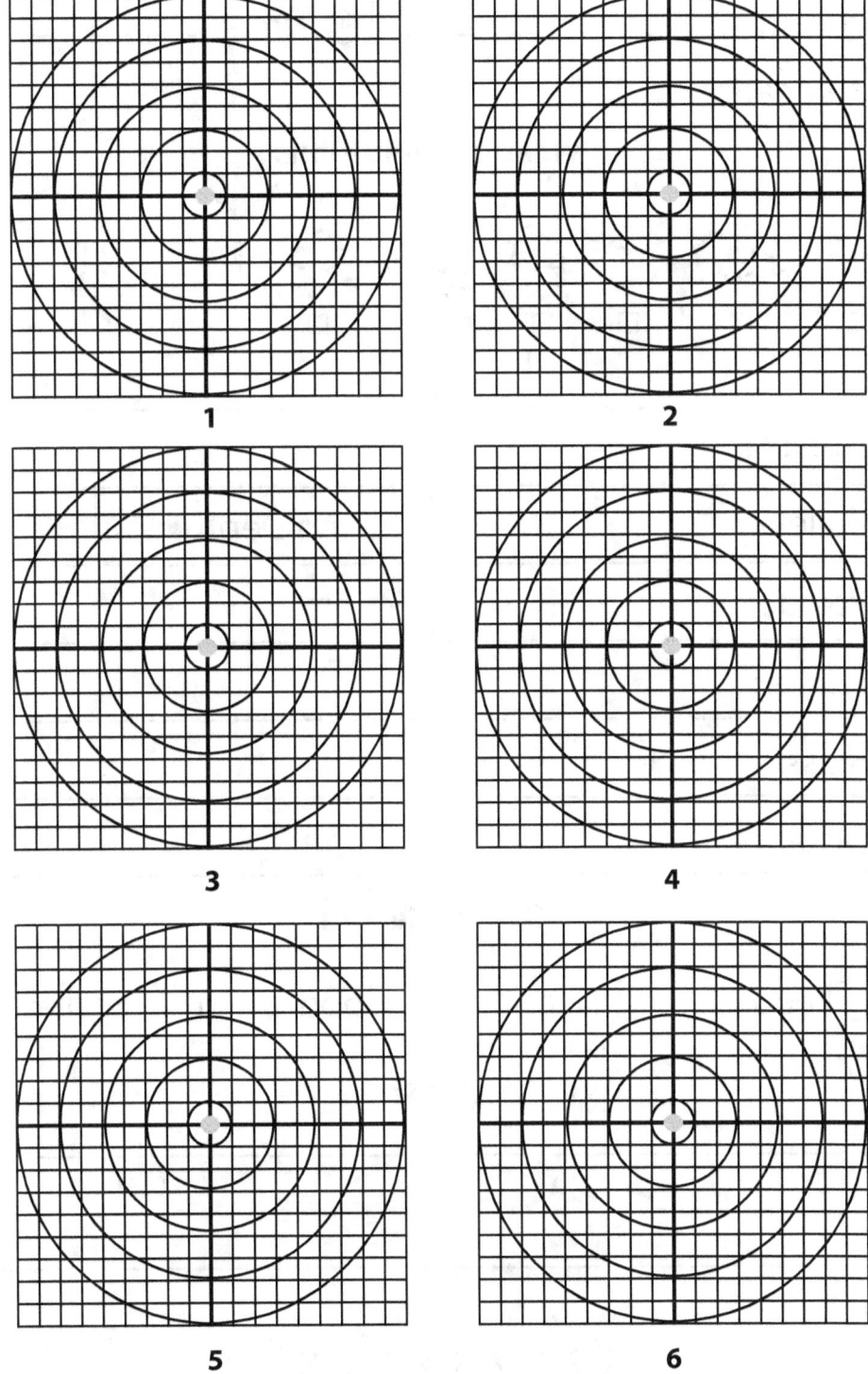

📅 Date: _____ 🕐 Time: _____

📍 Location: _____

Weather Conditions

☀️ ☐ ⛅ ☐ 🌤 ☐ 🌦 ☐ 🌧 ☐ 🌨 ☐ 🚩 _____ 🌡 _____

Firearm:	
Bullet:	Seating Depth:
Powder:	Grains:
Primer:	
Brass:	
Distance:	

Overall Results

☐ Poor   ☐ Fair   ☐ Good   ☐ Excellent

Notes

_____
_____
_____

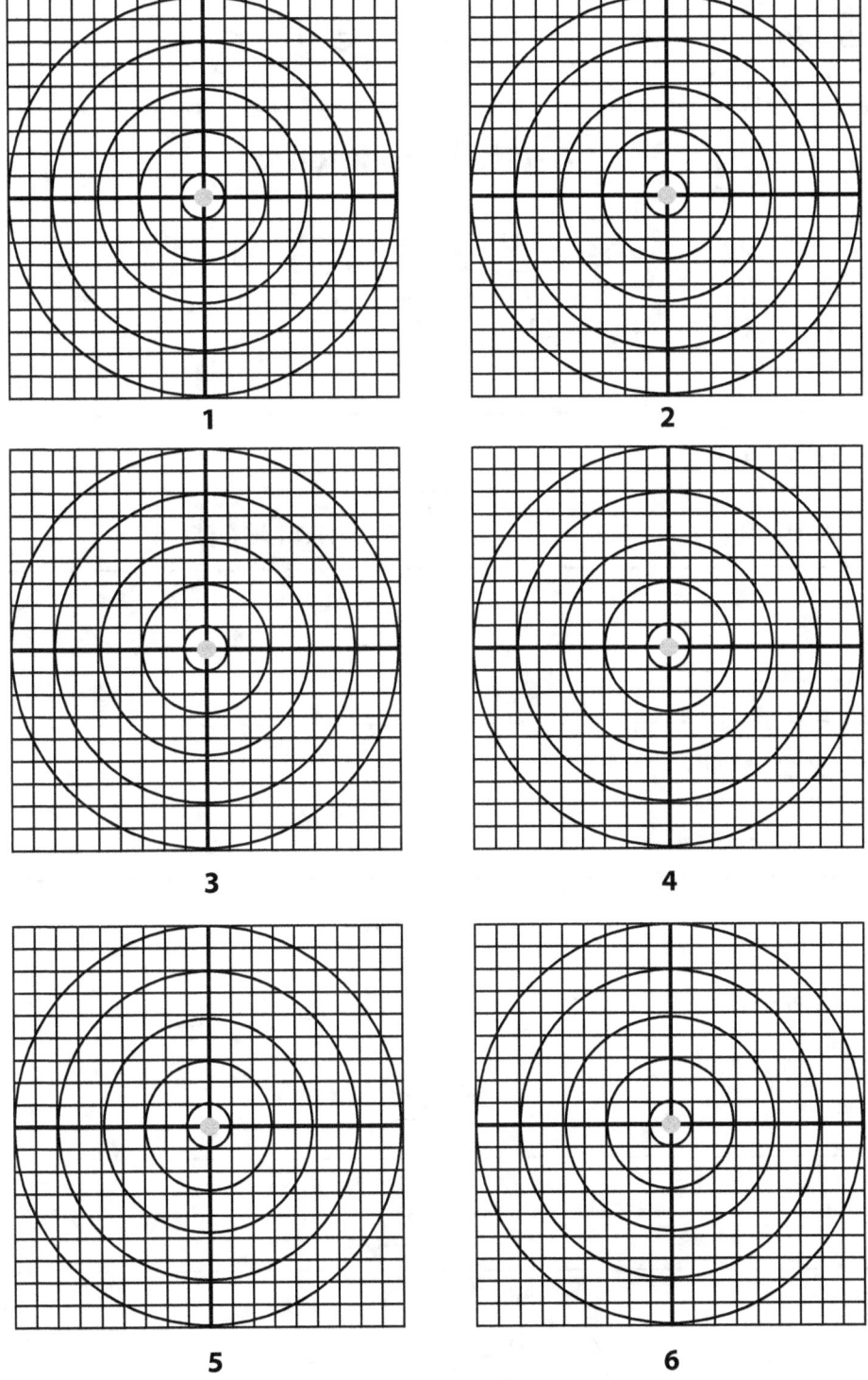

Date: _____ Time: _____

Location: _____

Weather Conditions

☀ ☁ ⛅ ☁ 🌧 🌨 🚩 🌡
☐ ☐ ☐ ☐ ☐ ☐ ___ ___

Firearm:	
Bullet:	Seating Depth:
Powder:	Grains:
Primer:	
Brass:	
Distance:	

Overall Results

☐ Poor   ☐ Fair   ☐ Good   ☐ Excellent

Notes

_____

_____

_____

☆ ☆ ☆ ☆ ☆

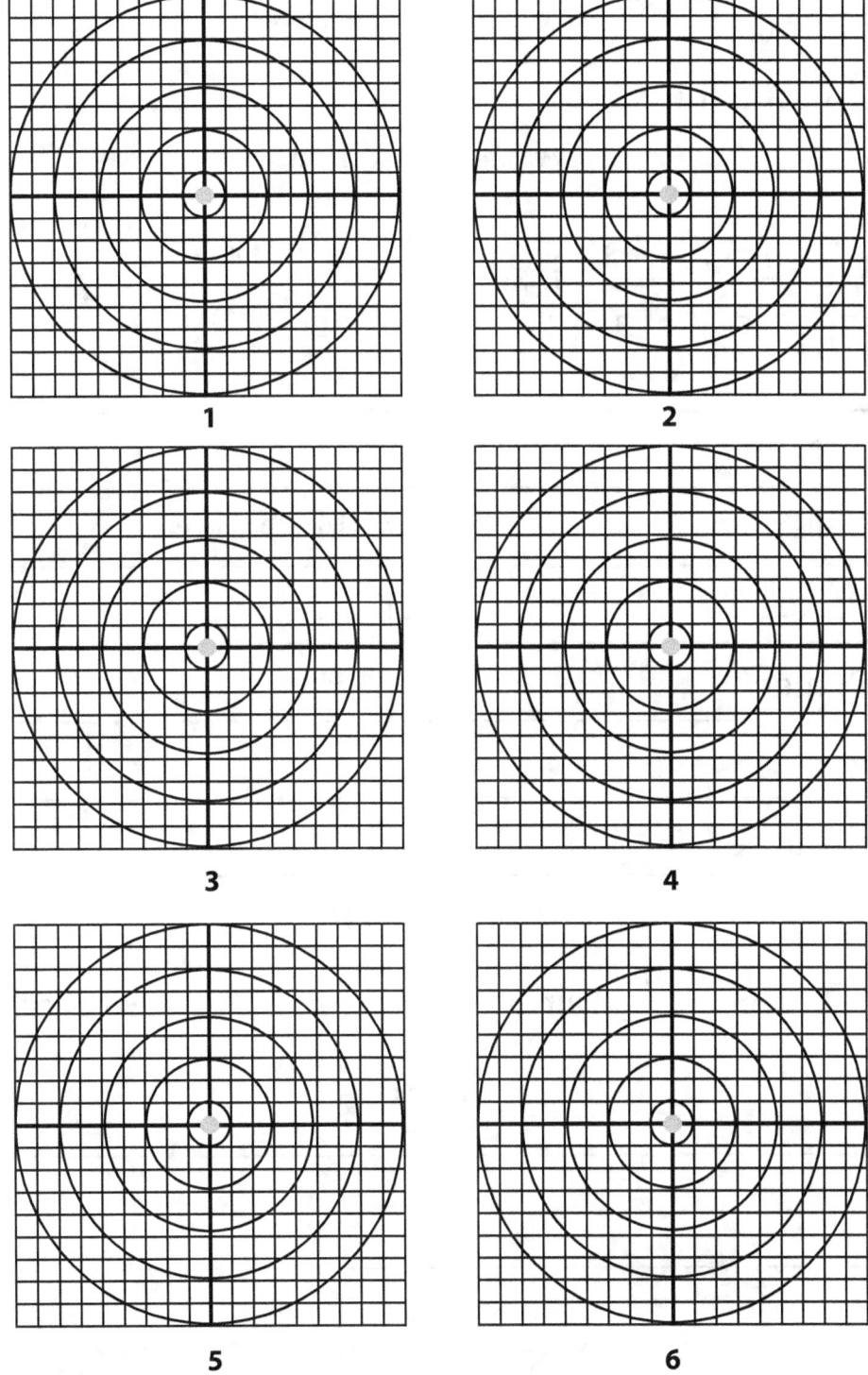

📅 Date: _____ 🕐 Time: _____

📍 Location: _____

Weather Conditions

☀️ ☁️ ⛅ 🌦️ 🌧️ 🌨️ 🚩 _____ 🌡️ _____

☐   ☐   ☐   ☐   ☐   ☐

Firearm:	
Bullet:	Seating Depth:
Powder:	Grains:
Primer:	
Brass:	
Distance:	

Overall Results

☐ Poor   ☐ Fair   ☐ Good   ☐ Excellent

Notes

_____

_____

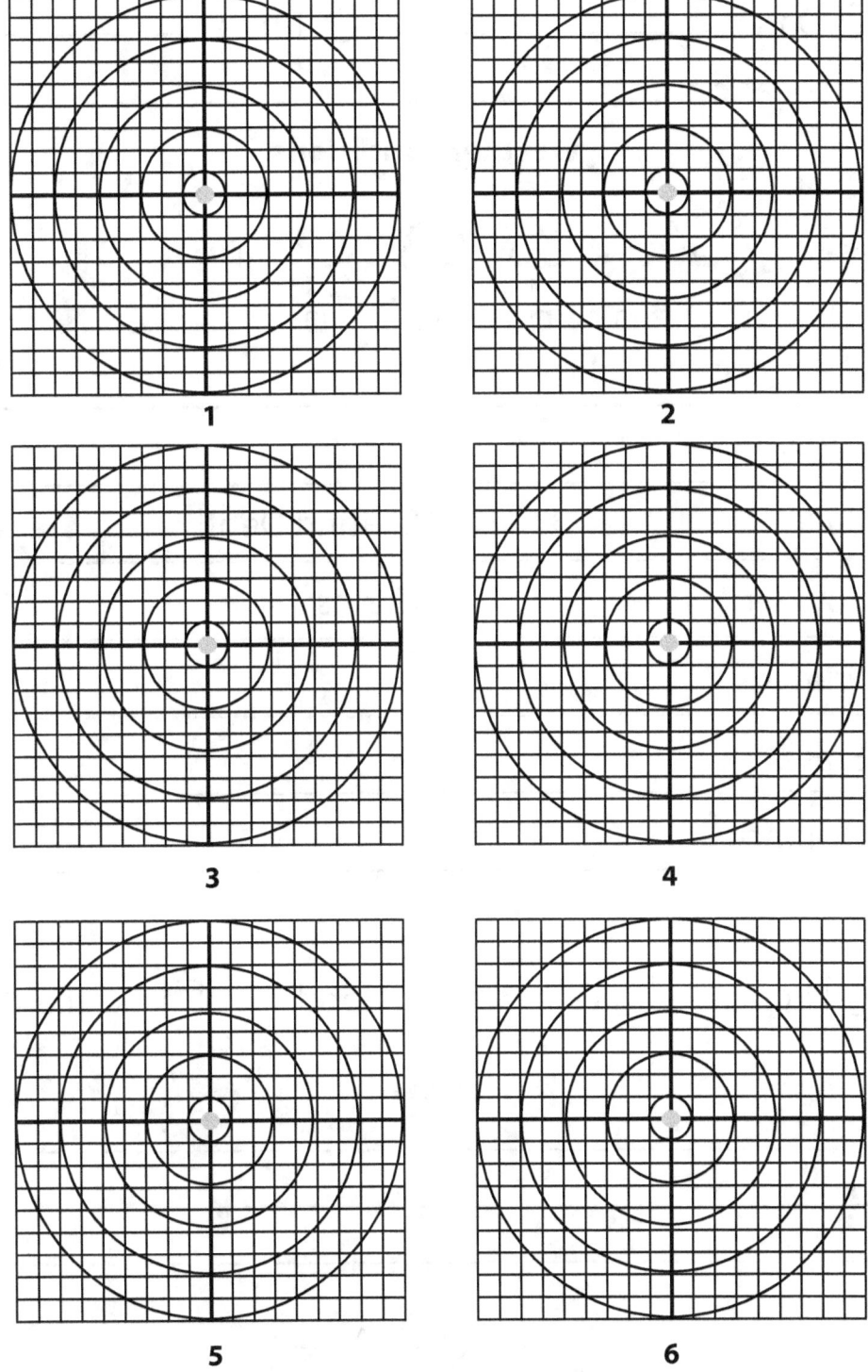

📅 Date: _____ 🕐 Time: _____

📍 Location: _____

Weather Conditions

☀️ ☁️ 🌤️ 🌧️ 🌧️ 🌨️ 🚩 _____ 🌡️ _____
☐   ☐   ☐   ☐   ☐   ☐

Firearm:	
Bullet:	Seating Depth:
Powder:	Grains:
Primer:	
Brass:	
Distance:	

Overall Results

☐ Poor   ☐ Fair   ☐ Good   ☐ Excellent

Notes

_____

_____

☆ ☆ ☆ ☆ ☆

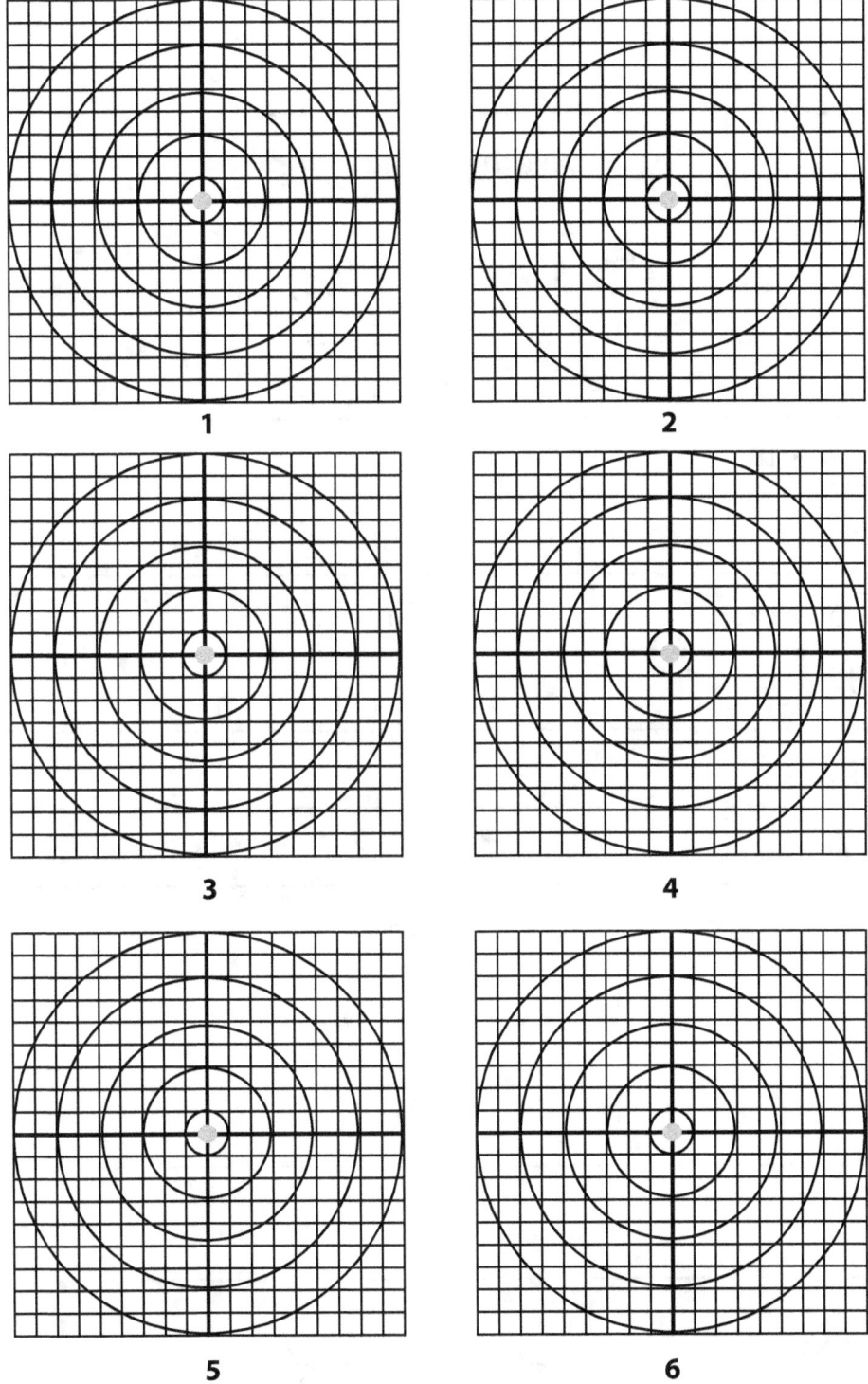

📅 Date: _____ 🕐 Time: _____

📍 Location: _____

Weather Conditions

☀️ ☁️ ⛅ 🌦️ 🌧️ 🌨️ 🚩 🌡️
☐ ☐ ☐ ☐ ☐ ☐ _____ _____

Firearm:	
Bullet:	Seating Depth:
Powder:	Grains:
Primer:	
Brass:	
Distance:	

Overall Results

☐ Poor ☐ Fair ☐ Good ☐ Excellent

Notes

_____
_____
_____

☆ ☆ ☆ ☆ ☆

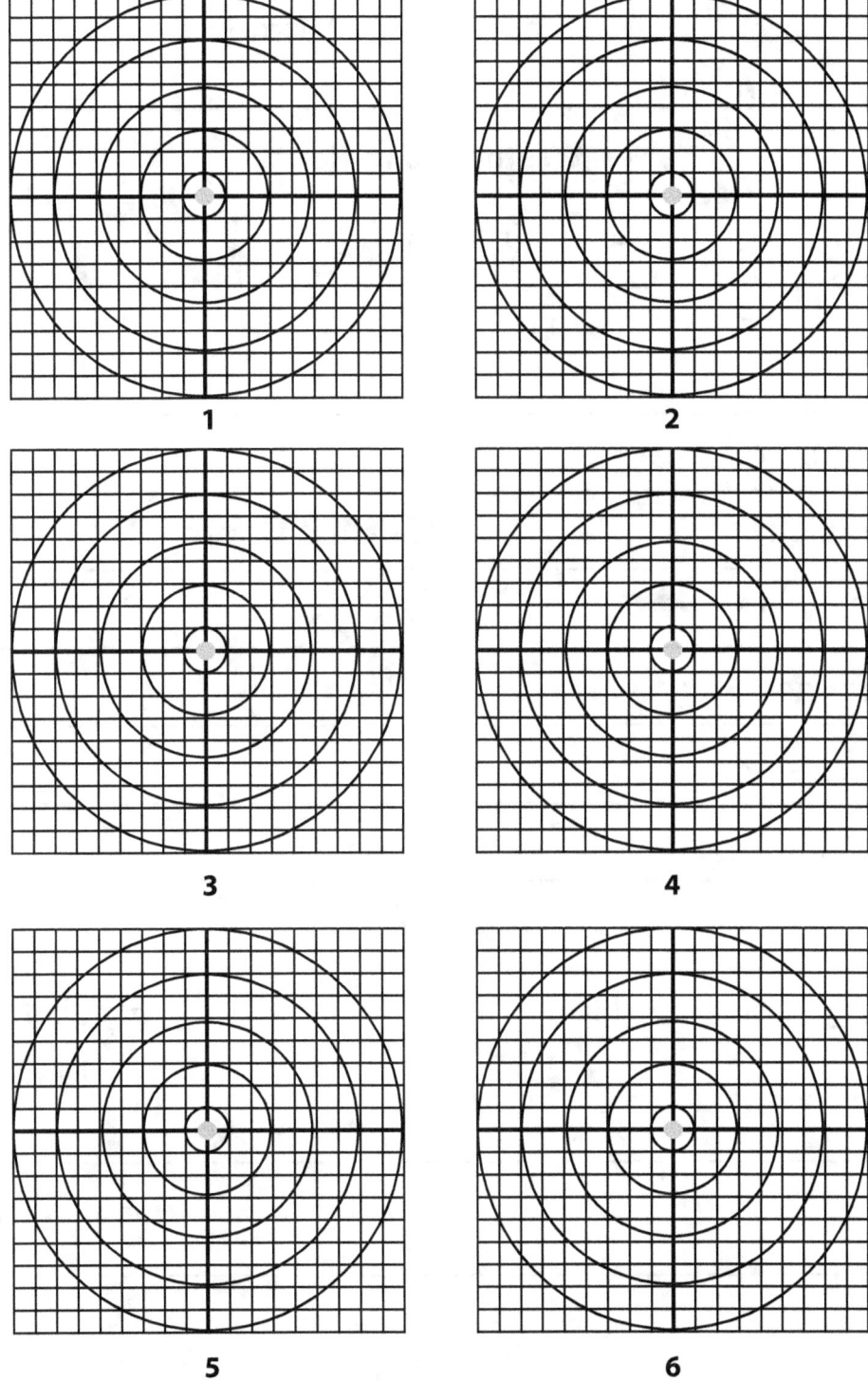

📅 Date: _____ 🕐 Time: _____

📍 Location: _____

Weather Conditions

☀️ ☁️ ⛅ ☁️ 🌧️ 🌨️ 🚩 🌡️
☐ ☐ ☐ ☐ ☐ ☐

Firearm:	
Bullet:	Seating Depth:
Powder:	Grains:
Primer:	
Brass:	
Distance:	

Overall Results

☐ Poor   ☐ Fair   ☐ Good   ☐ Excellent

Notes

_____
_____
_____

☆ ☆ ☆ ☆ ☆

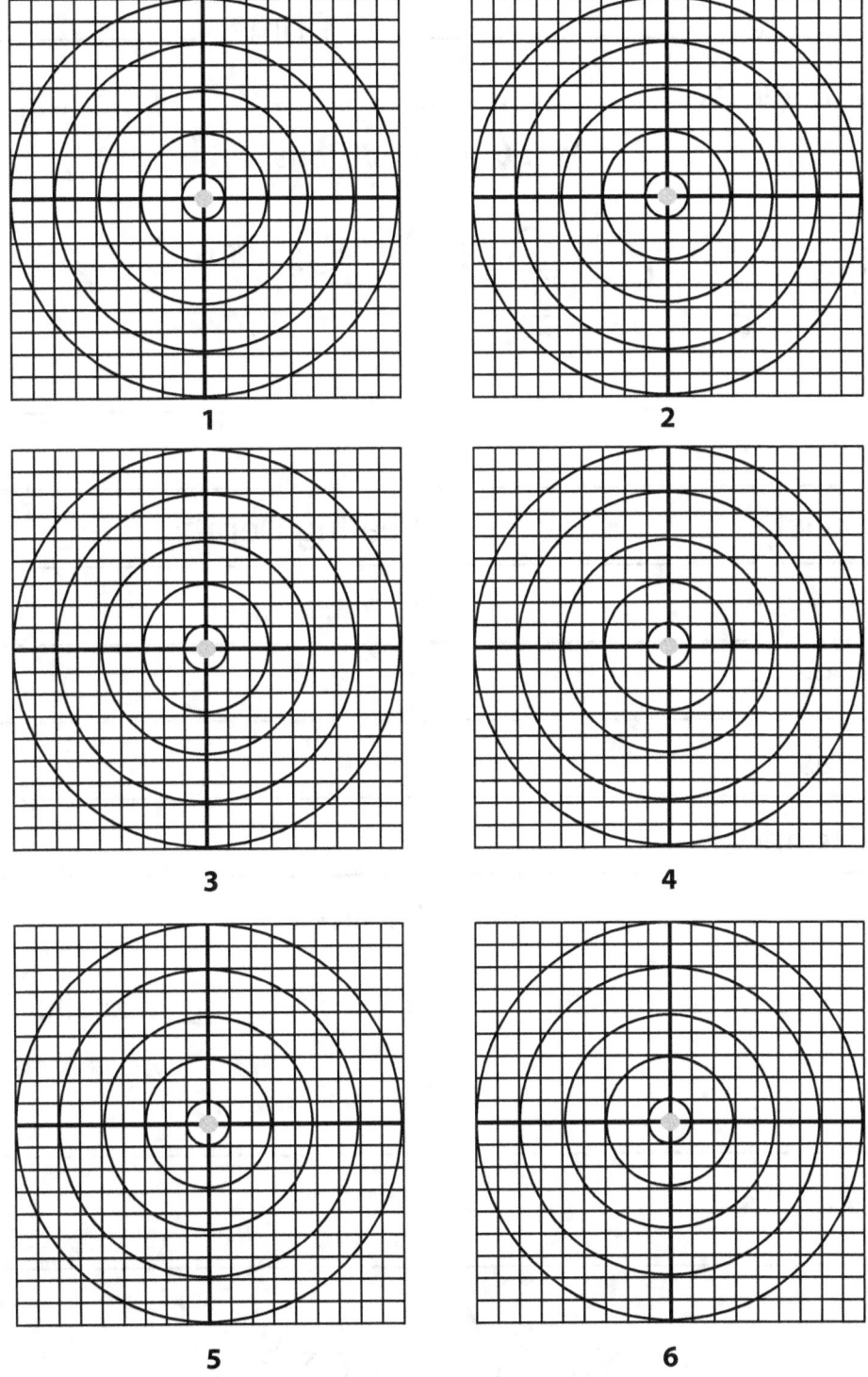

Date: _____ Time: _____

Location: _____

Weather Conditions

☀ ☁ ⛅ 🌧 🌧 🌨 ⚑ 🌡
☐ ☐ ☐ ☐ ☐ ☐

Firearm:	
Bullet:	Seating Depth:
Powder:	Grains:
Primer:	
Brass:	
Distance:	

Overall Results

☐ Poor   ☐ Fair   ☐ Good   ☐ Excellent

Notes

_____

_____

_____

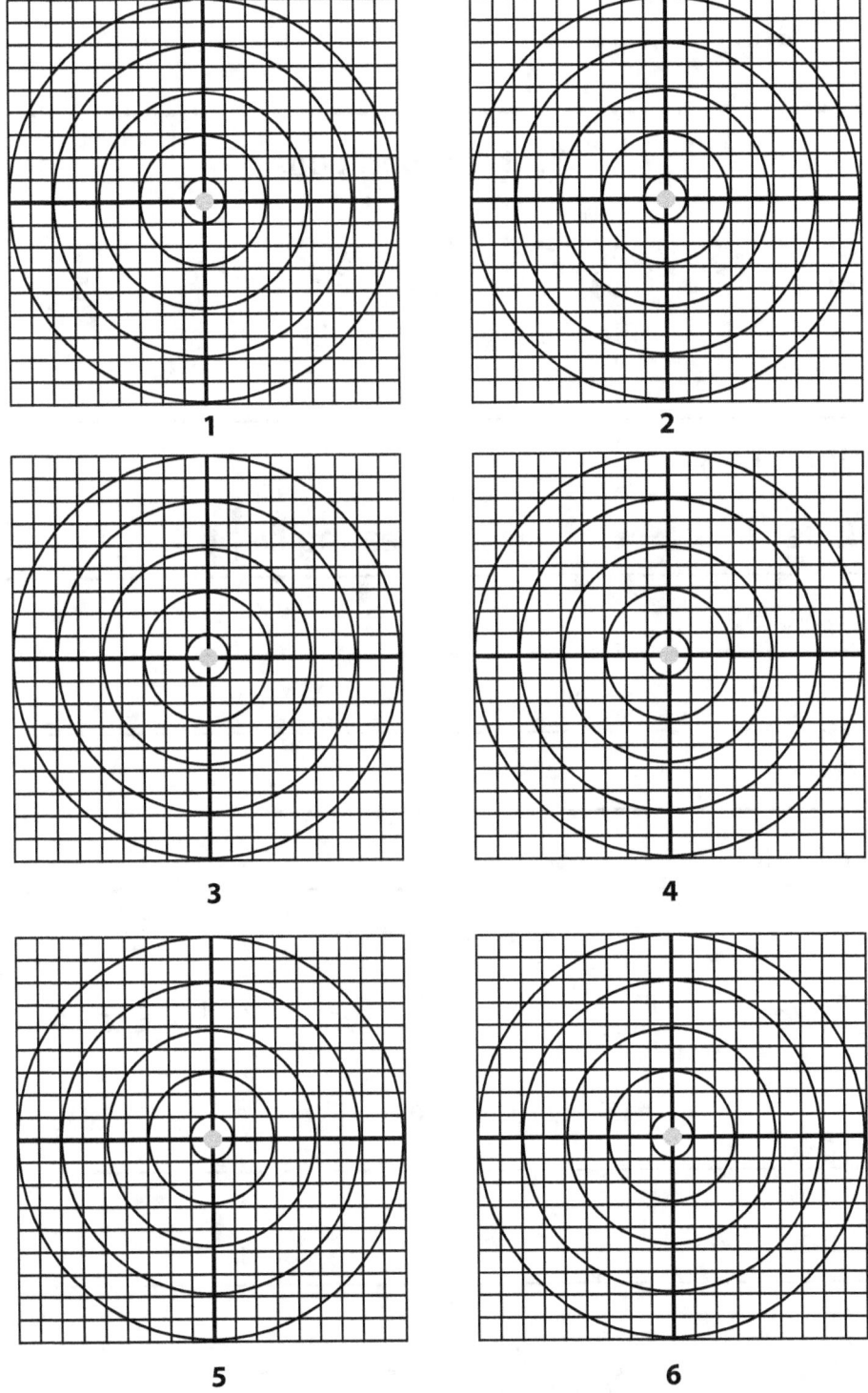

Date: _____ Time: _____

 Location: _____

Weather Conditions

☀ ☁ ⛅ 🌧 🌧 🌨 ⚑ _____ 🌡 _____
☐ ☐ ☐ ☐ ☐ ☐

Firearm:	
Bullet:	Seating Depth:
Powder:	Grains:
Primer:	
Brass:	
Distance:	

Overall Results

☐ Poor   ☐ Fair   ☐ Good   ☐ Excellent

Notes

_____
_____
_____

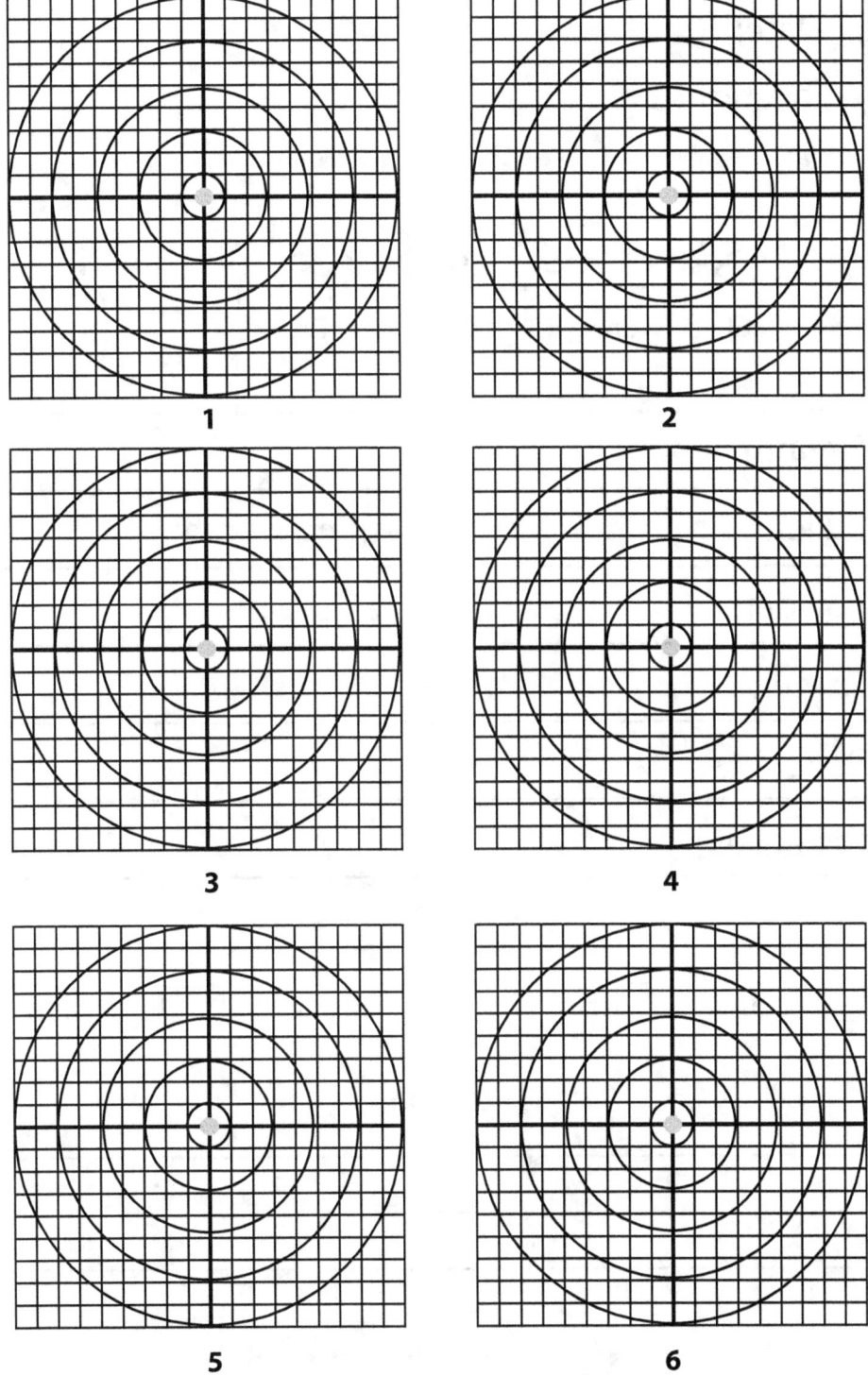

📅 Date: _____ 🕐 Time: _____

📍 Location: _____

Weather Conditions

☀️ ☁️ ⛅ 🌥️ 🌧️ 🌨️ 🚩 🌡️
☐   ☐   ☐   ☐   ☐   ☐

Firearm:	
Bullet:	Seating Depth:
Powder:	Grains:
Primer:	
Brass:	
Distance:	

Overall Results

☐ Poor   ☐ Fair   ☐ Good   ☐ Excellent

Notes

_____

_____

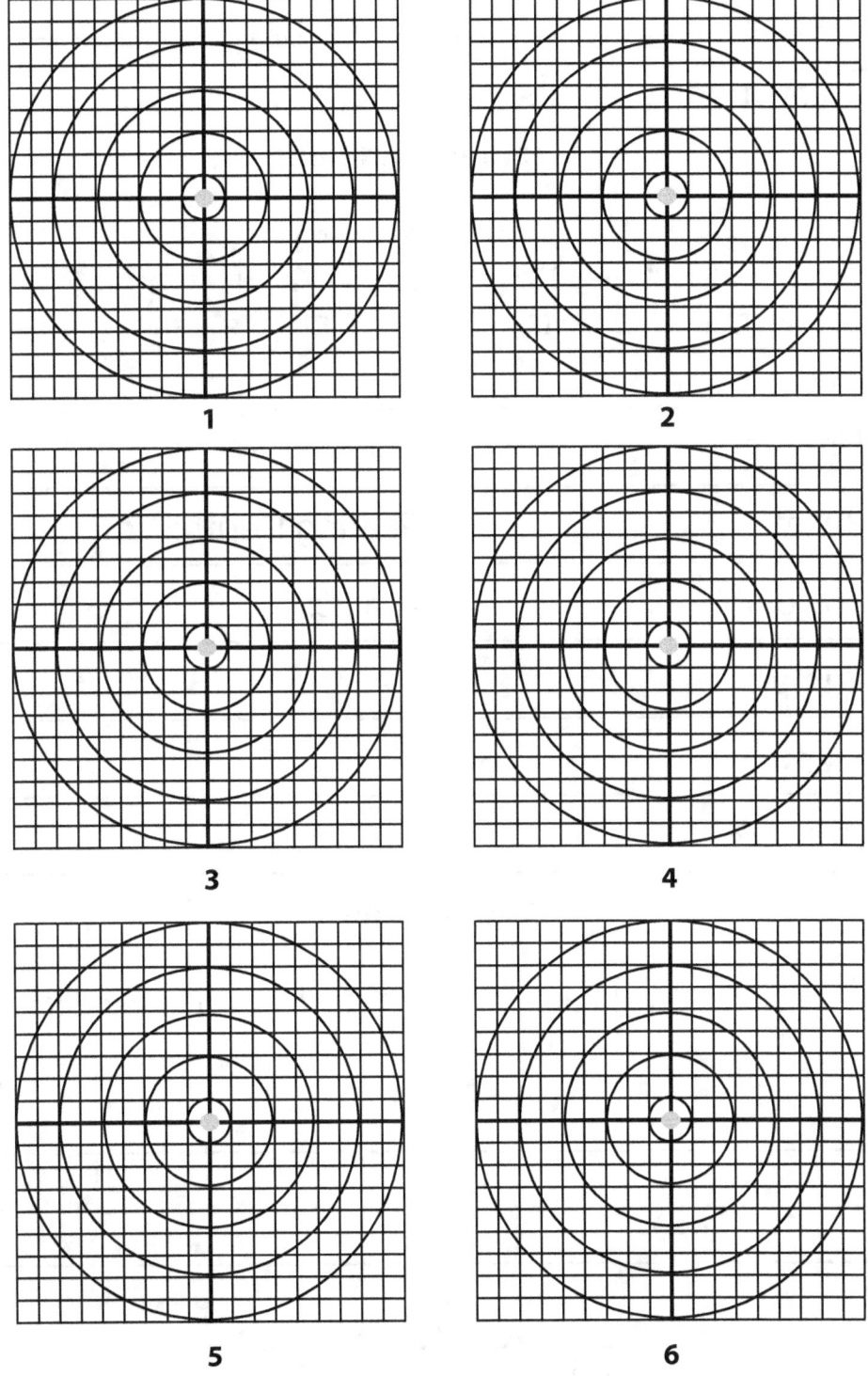

📅 Date: _____ 🕐 Time: _____

📍 Location: _____

Weather Conditions

☀ ☁ ⛅ 🌧 🌧 🌨 🚩 🌡 _____
☐   ☐   ☐   ☐   ☐   ☐

Firearm:	
Bullet:	Seating Depth:
Powder:	Grains:
Primer:	
Brass:	
Distance:	

Overall Results

☐ Poor   ☐ Fair   ☐ Good   ☐ Excellent

Notes

_____

_____

_____

☆ ☆ ☆ ☆ ☆

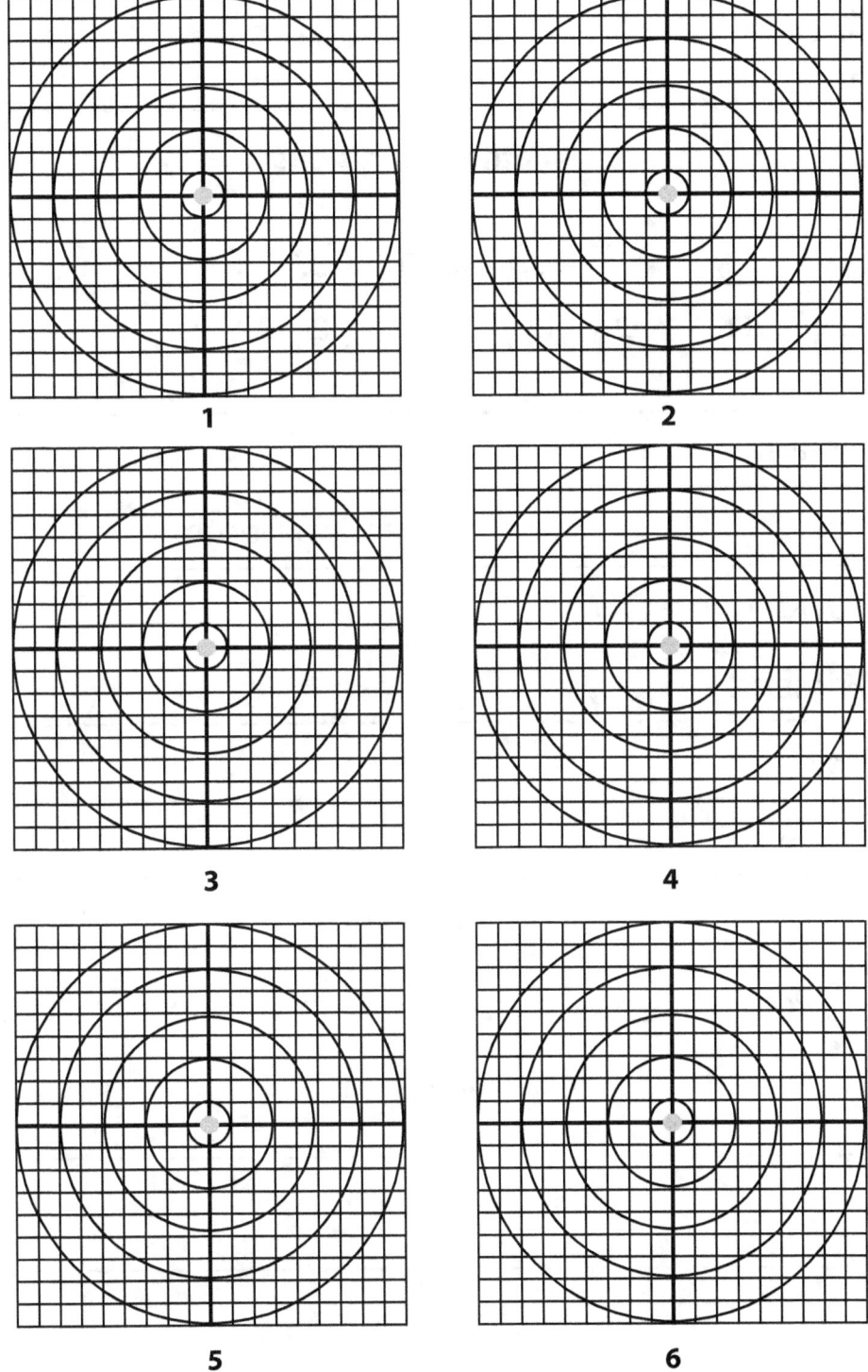

Date: _____ Time: _____

Location: _____

Weather Conditions

☀ ☁ ⛅ 🌧 🌧 🌨 🚩 🌡
☐ ☐ ☐ ☐ ☐ ☐   _____ _____

Firearm:	
Bullet:	Seating Depth:
Powder:	Grains:
Primer:	
Brass:	
Distance:	

Overall Results

☐ Poor   ☐ Fair   ☐ Good   ☐ Excellent

Notes

_____
_____
_____

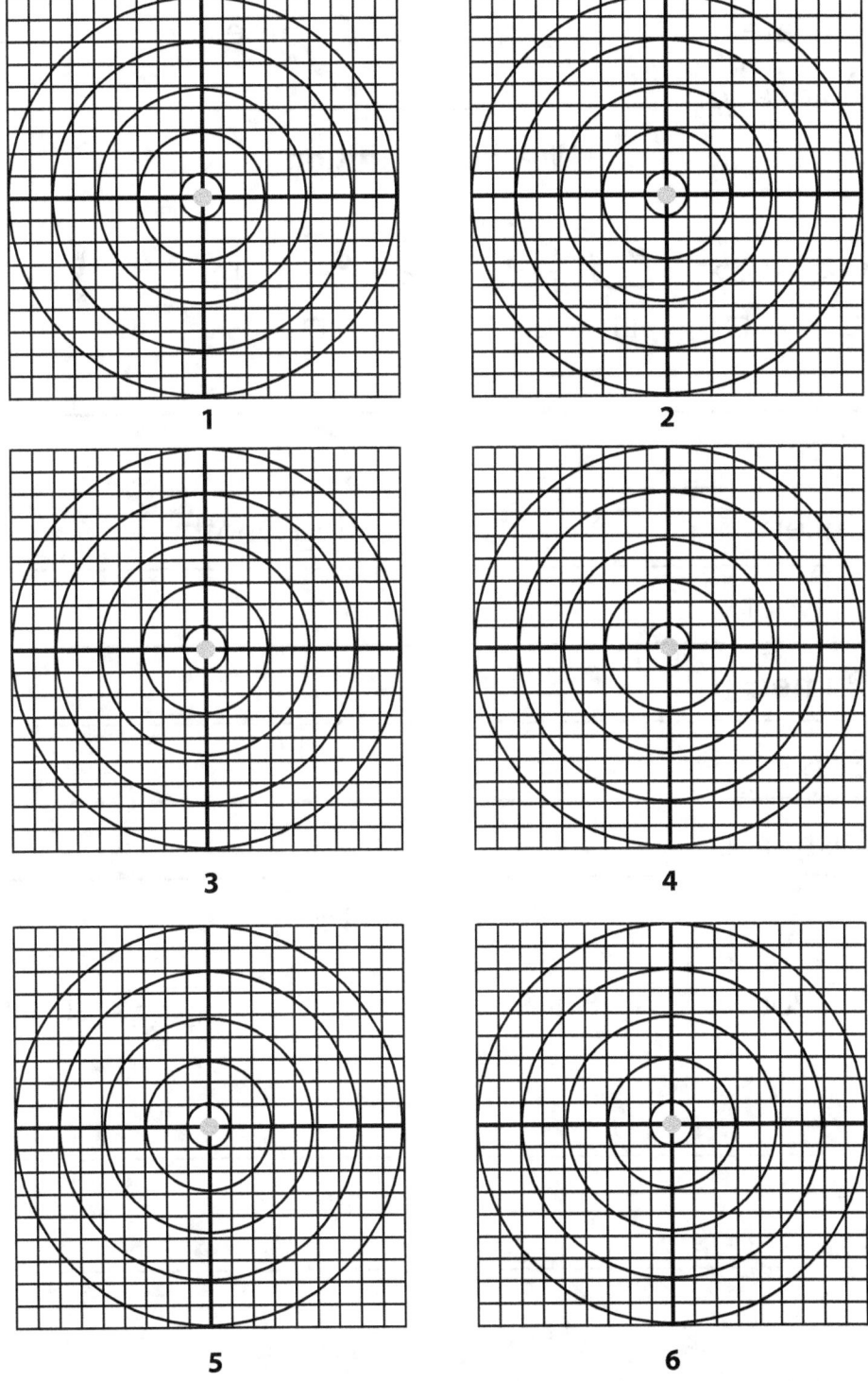

📅 Date: _____   🕐 Time: _____
📍 Location: _____

Weather Conditions

☀ ☁ 🌥 🌦 🌧 🌨 🚩 _____ 🌡 _____
☐ ☐ ☐ ☐ ☐ ☐

Firearm:	
Bullet:	Seating Depth:
Powder:	Grains:
Primer:	
Brass:	
Distance:	

Overall Results

☐ Poor   ☐ Fair   ☐ Good   ☐ Excellent

Notes

_____
_____
_____

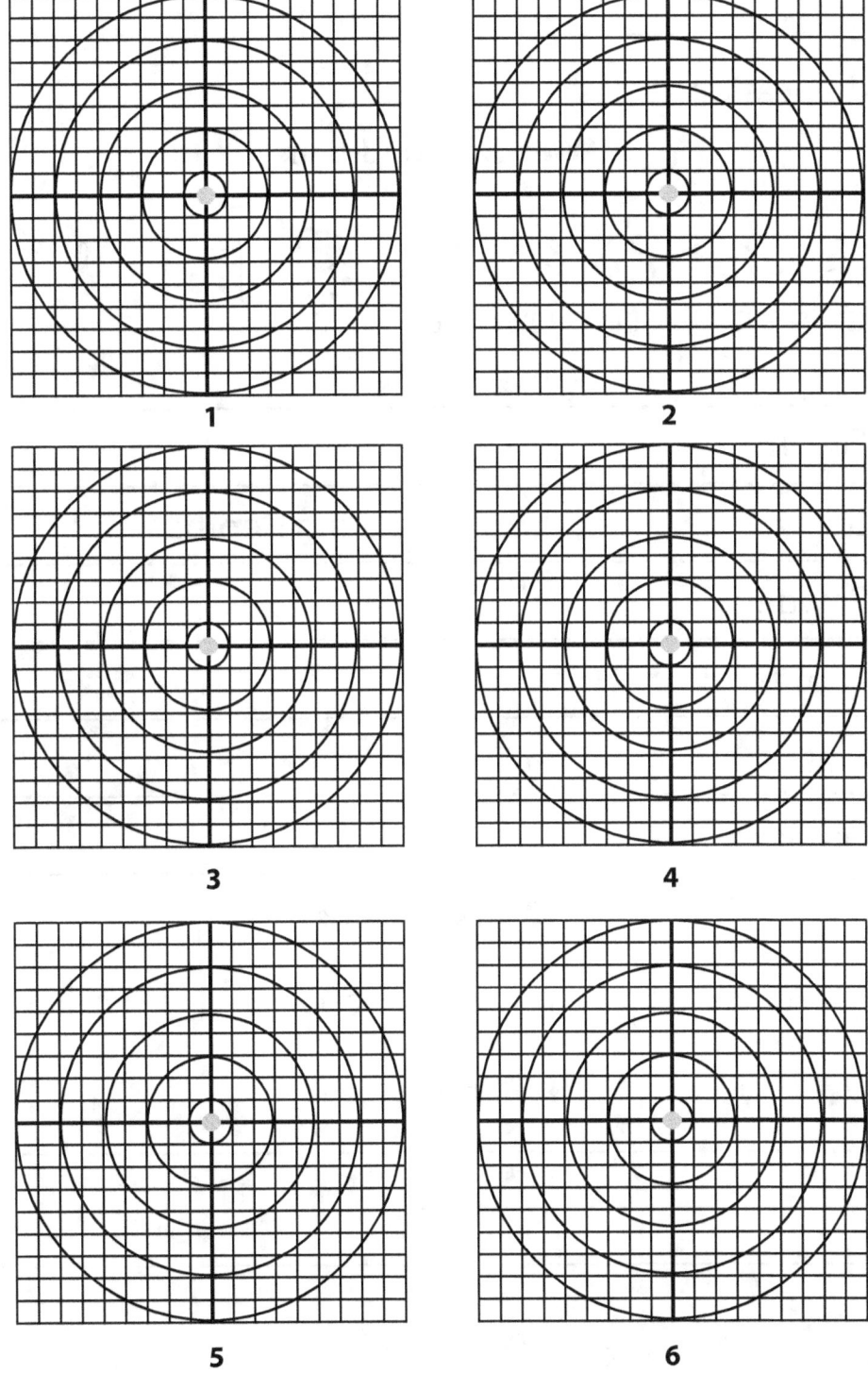

📅 Date: _____ 🕐 Time: _____

📍 Location: _____

Weather Conditions

☀️ ☐   ☁️ ☐   🌤️ ☐   🌧️ ☐   🌧️ ☐   🌨️ ☐   🚩 _____   🌡️ _____

Firearm:	
Bullet:	Seating Depth:
Powder:	Grains:
Primer:	
Brass:	
Distance:	

Overall Results

☐ Poor   ☐ Fair   ☐ Good   ☐ Excellent

Notes

_____

_____

_____

☆ ☆ ☆ ☆ ☆

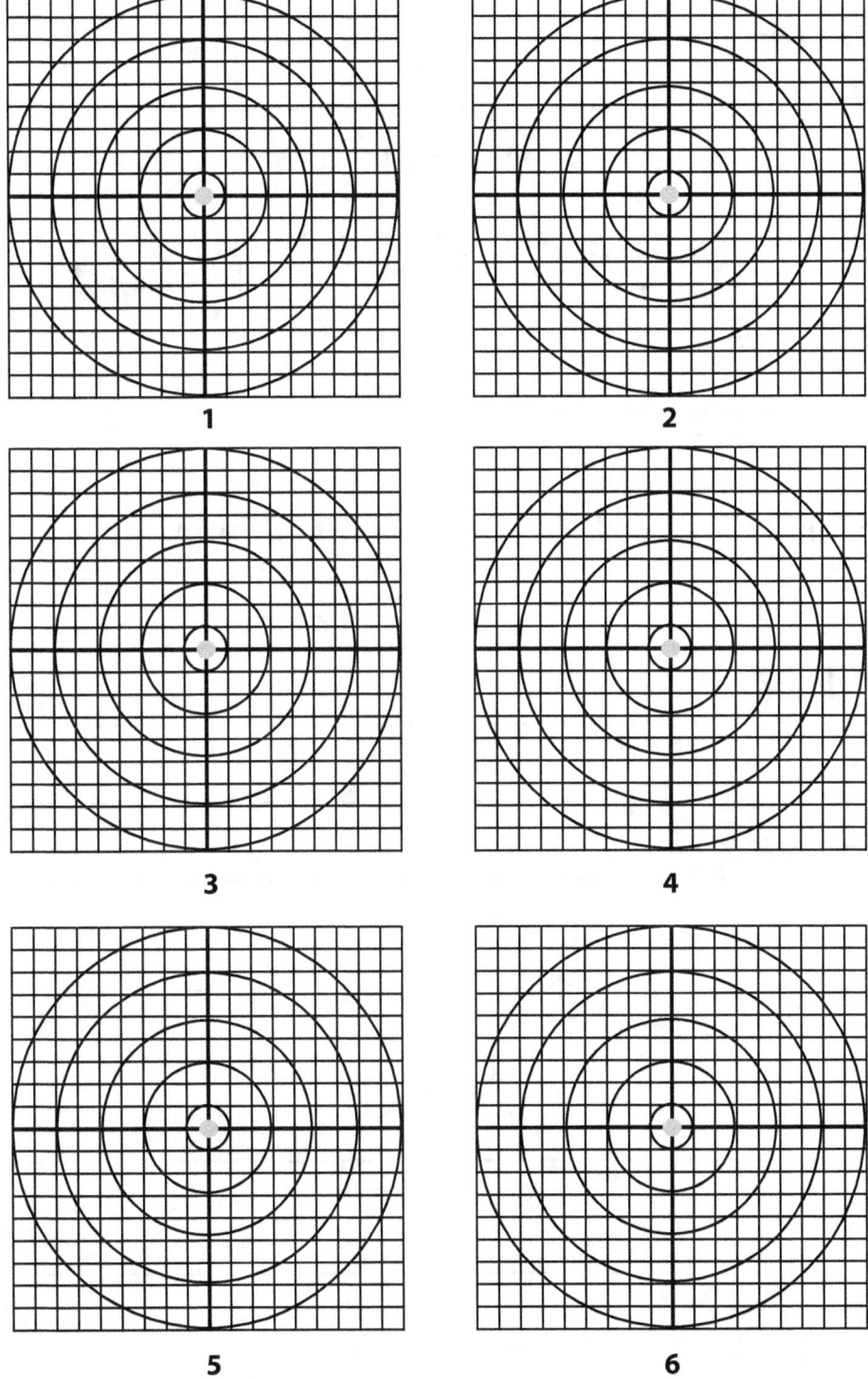

📅 Date: _____ 🕐 Time: _____

📍 Location: _____

Weather Conditions

☀ ☁ 🌤 ⛅ 🌧 🌨 🚩 🌡 _____

☐ ☐ ☐ ☐ ☐ ☐

Firearm:	
Bullet:	Seating Depth:
Powder:	Grains:
Primer:	
Brass:	
Distance:	

Overall Results

☐ Poor   ☐ Fair   ☐ Good   ☐ Excellent

Notes

_____

_____

_____

☆ ☆ ☆ ☆ ☆

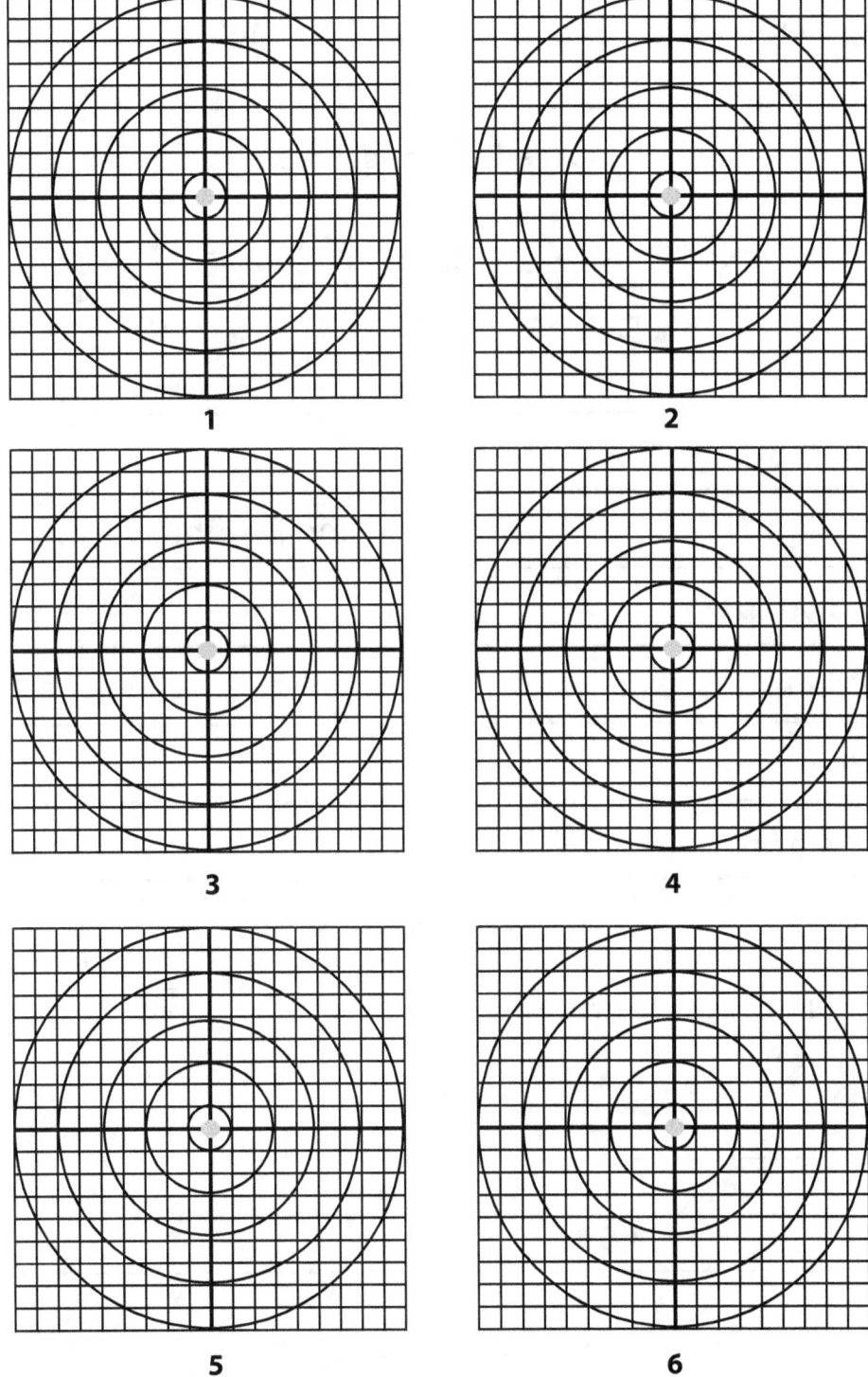

📅 Date: _____ 🕐 Time: _____

📍 Location: _____

Weather Conditions

☀️ ☁️ 🌤️ 🌧️ 🌦️ 🌨️ 🚩 _____ 🌡️ _____
☐   ☐   ☐   ☐   ☐   ☐

Firearm:	
Bullet:	Seating Depth:
Powder:	Grains:
Primer:	
Brass:	
Distance:	

Overall Results

☐ Poor   ☐ Fair   ☐ Good   ☐ Excellent

Notes

_____

_____

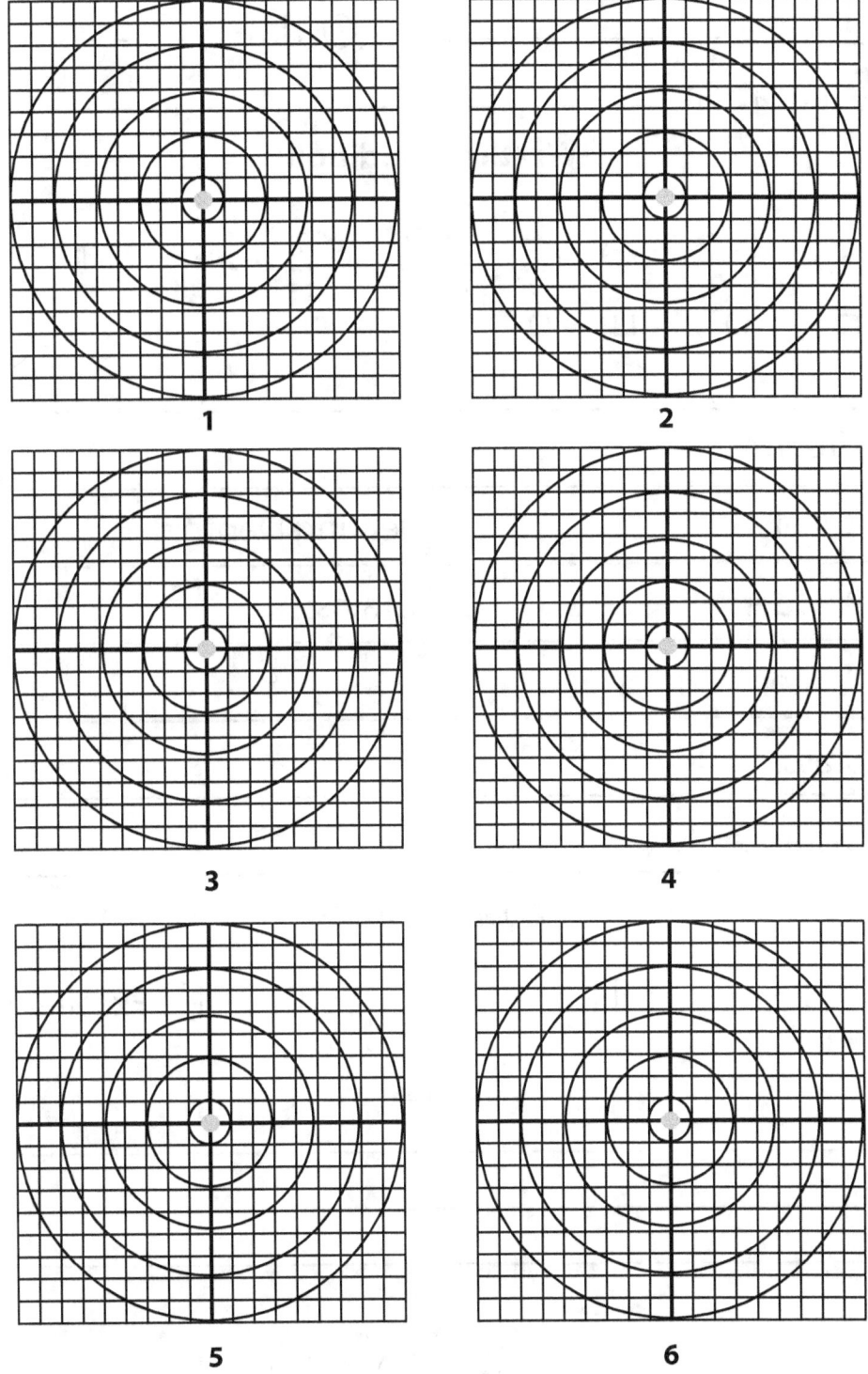

📅 Date: _____ 🕐 Time: _____

📍 Location: _____

Weather Conditions

☀ ☁ ⛅ 🌧 🌧 🌨 🚩 🌡
☐ ☐ ☐ ☐ ☐ ☐ ____ ____

Firearm:	
Bullet:	Seating Depth:
Powder:	Grains:
Primer:	
Brass:	
Distance:	

Overall Results

☐ Poor   ☐ Fair   ☐ Good   ☐ Excellent

Notes

_____
_____
_____

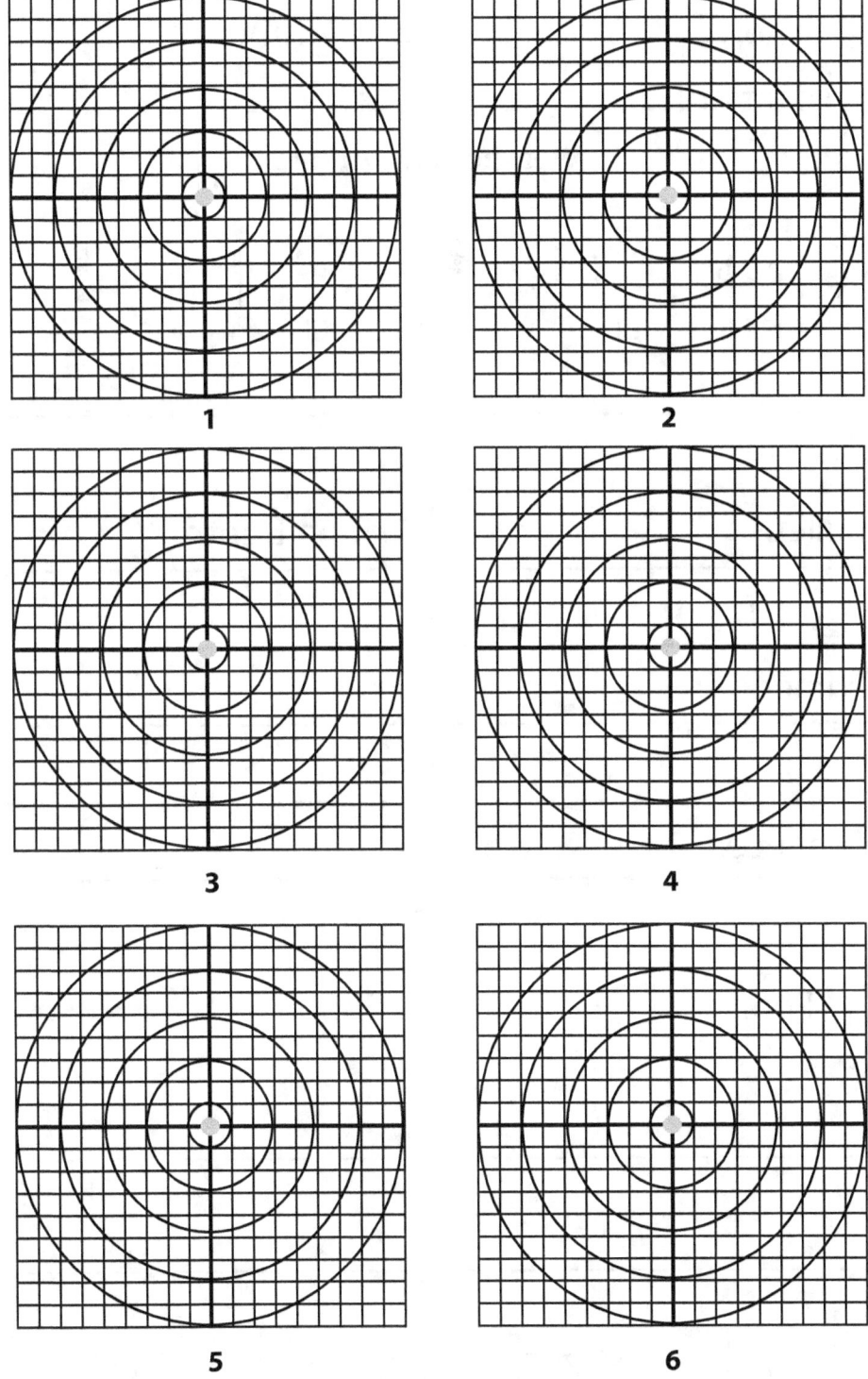

📅 Date: _____ 🕐 Time: _____

📍 Location: _____

Weather Conditions

☀ ☁ ⛅ 🌥 🌧 🌨 🚩 🌡
☐ ☐ ☐ ☐ ☐ ☐

Firearm:	
Bullet:	Seating Depth:
Powder:	Grains:
Primer:	
Brass:	
Distance:	

Overall Results

☐ Poor   ☐ Fair   ☐ Good   ☐ Excellent

Notes

_____

_____

_____

☆ ☆ ☆ ☆ ☆

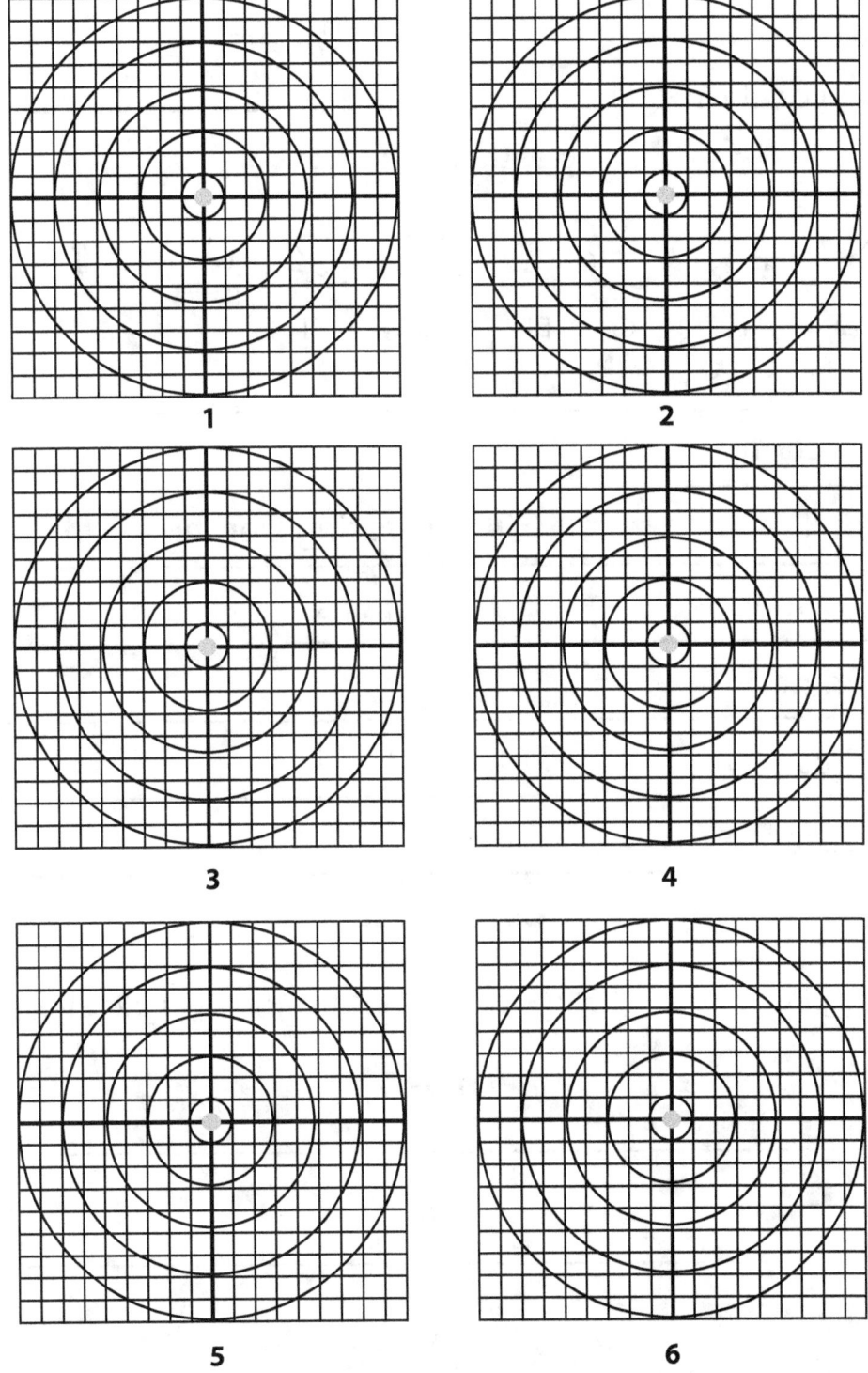

📅 Date: _____ 🕐 Time: _____

📍 Location: _____

Weather Conditions

☀️ ☁️ 🌤️ 🌧️ 🌦️ 🌨️ 🚩 🌡️
☐ ☐ ☐ ☐ ☐ ☐

Firearm:	
Bullet:	Seating Depth:
Powder:	Grains:
Primer:	
Brass:	
Distance:	

Overall Results

☐ Poor   ☐ Fair   ☐ Good   ☐ Excellent

Notes

_____

_____

_____

☆ ☆ ☆ ☆ ☆

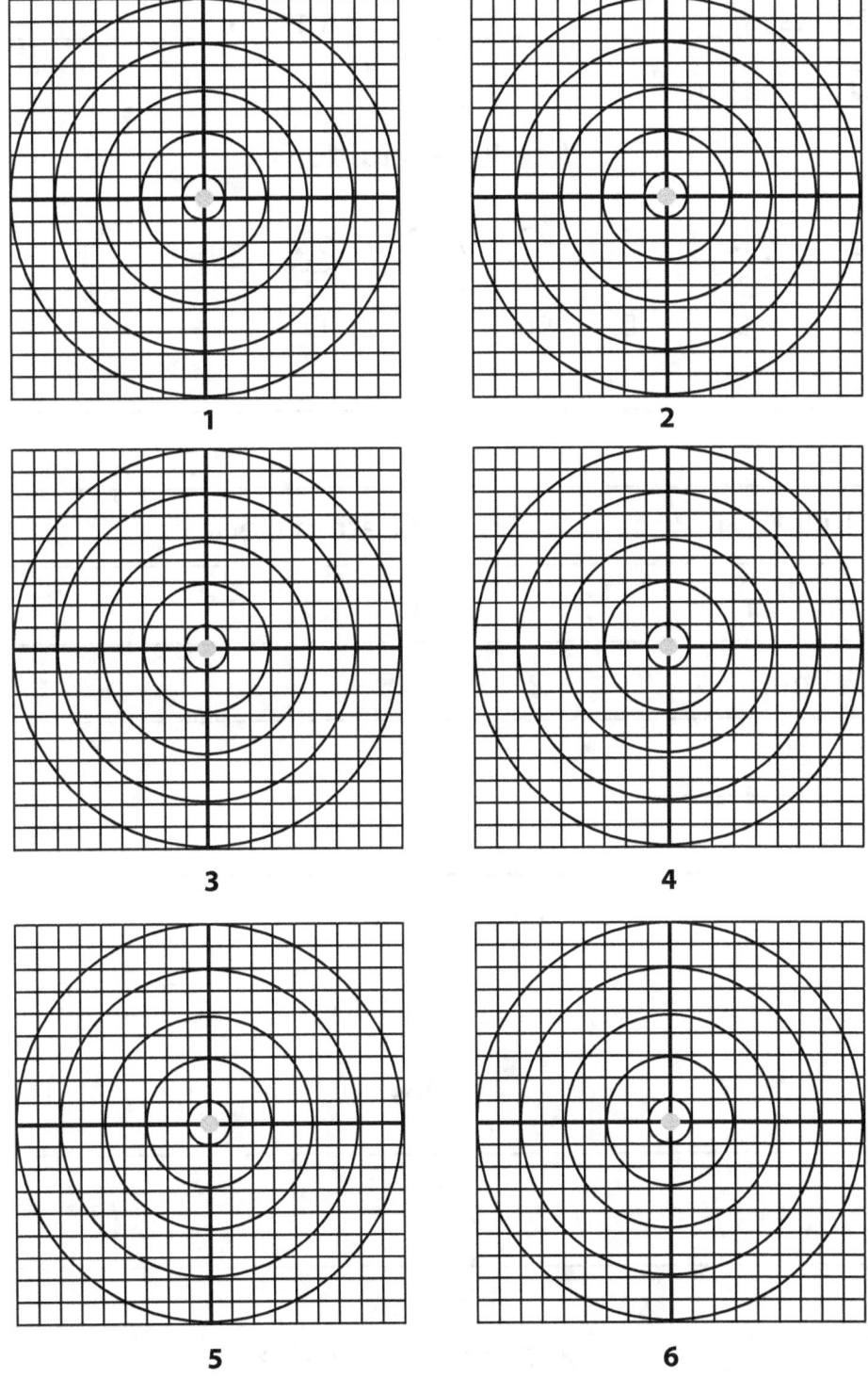

📅 Date: _____   🕐 Time: _____

📍 Location: _____

Weather Conditions

☀️ ☁️ ⛅ 🌧️ 🌧️ 🌨️ 🚩 🌡️
☐   ☐   ☐   ☐   ☐   ☐   ____ ____

Firearm:	
Bullet:	Seating Depth:
Powder:	Grains:
Primer:	
Brass:	
Distance:	

Overall Results

☐ Poor   ☐ Fair   ☐ Good   ☐ Excellent

Notes

_____
_____
_____

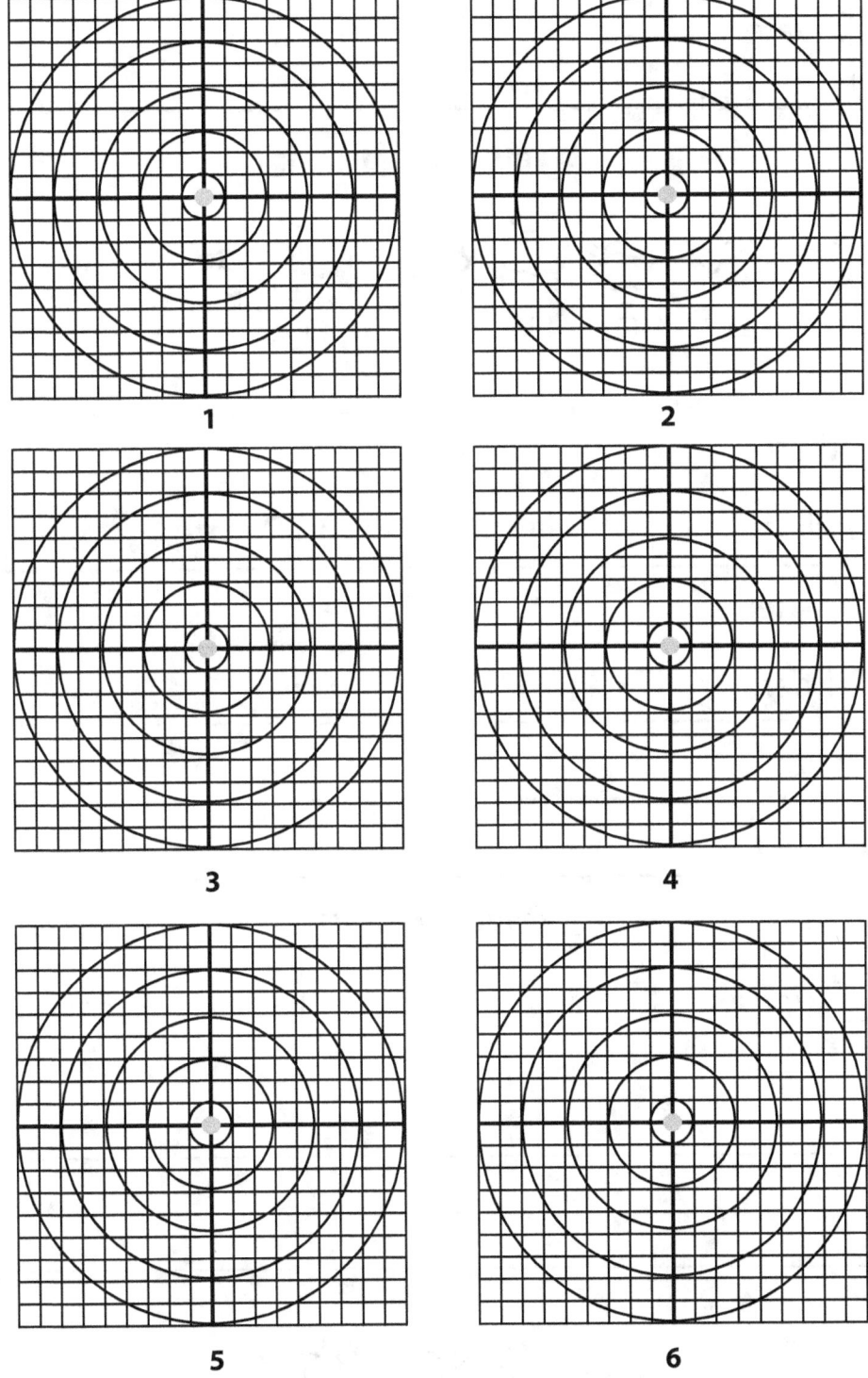

📅 Date: _____ 🕐 Time: _____

📍 Location: _____

Weather Conditions

☀️ ☁️ ⛅ 🌧️ 🌧️ 🌨️ 🚩 _____ 🌡️ _____
☐ ☐ ☐ ☐ ☐ ☐

Firearm:	
Bullet:	Seating Depth:
Powder:	Grains:
Primer:	
Brass:	
Distance:	

Overall Results

☐ Poor   ☐ Fair   ☐ Good   ☐ Excellent

Notes

_____

_____

☆ ☆ ☆ ☆ ☆

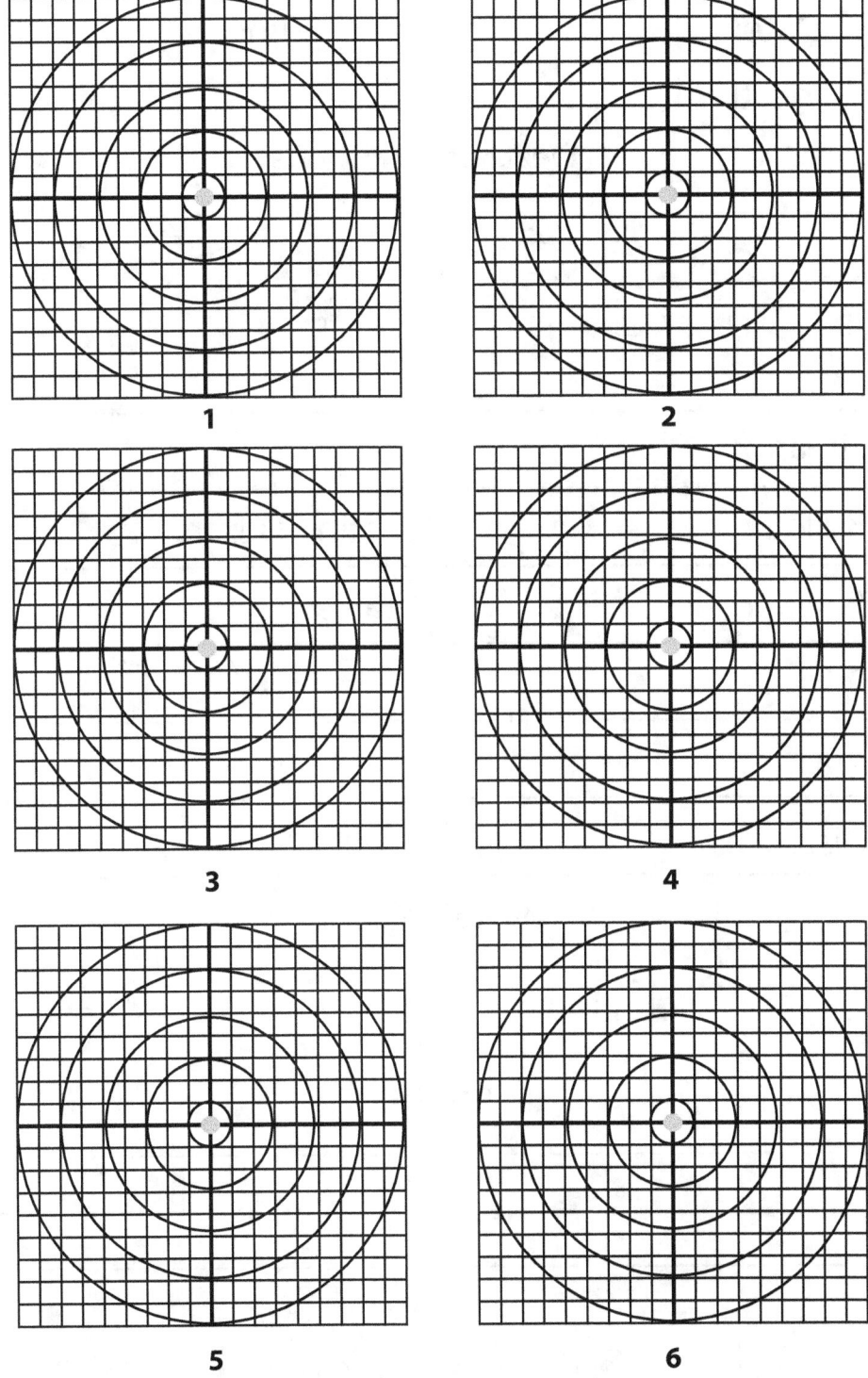

📅 Date: _____ 🕐 Time: _____

📍 Location: _____

Weather Conditions

☀️ ☁️ ⛅ 🌦️ 🌧️ 🌨️ 🚩 _____ 🌡️ _____

☐   ☐   ☐   ☐   ☐   ☐

Firearm:	
Bullet:	Seating Depth:
Powder:	Grains:
Primer:	
Brass:	
Distance:	

Overall Results

☐ Poor   ☐ Fair   ☐ Good   ☐ Excellent

Notes

_____

_____

_____

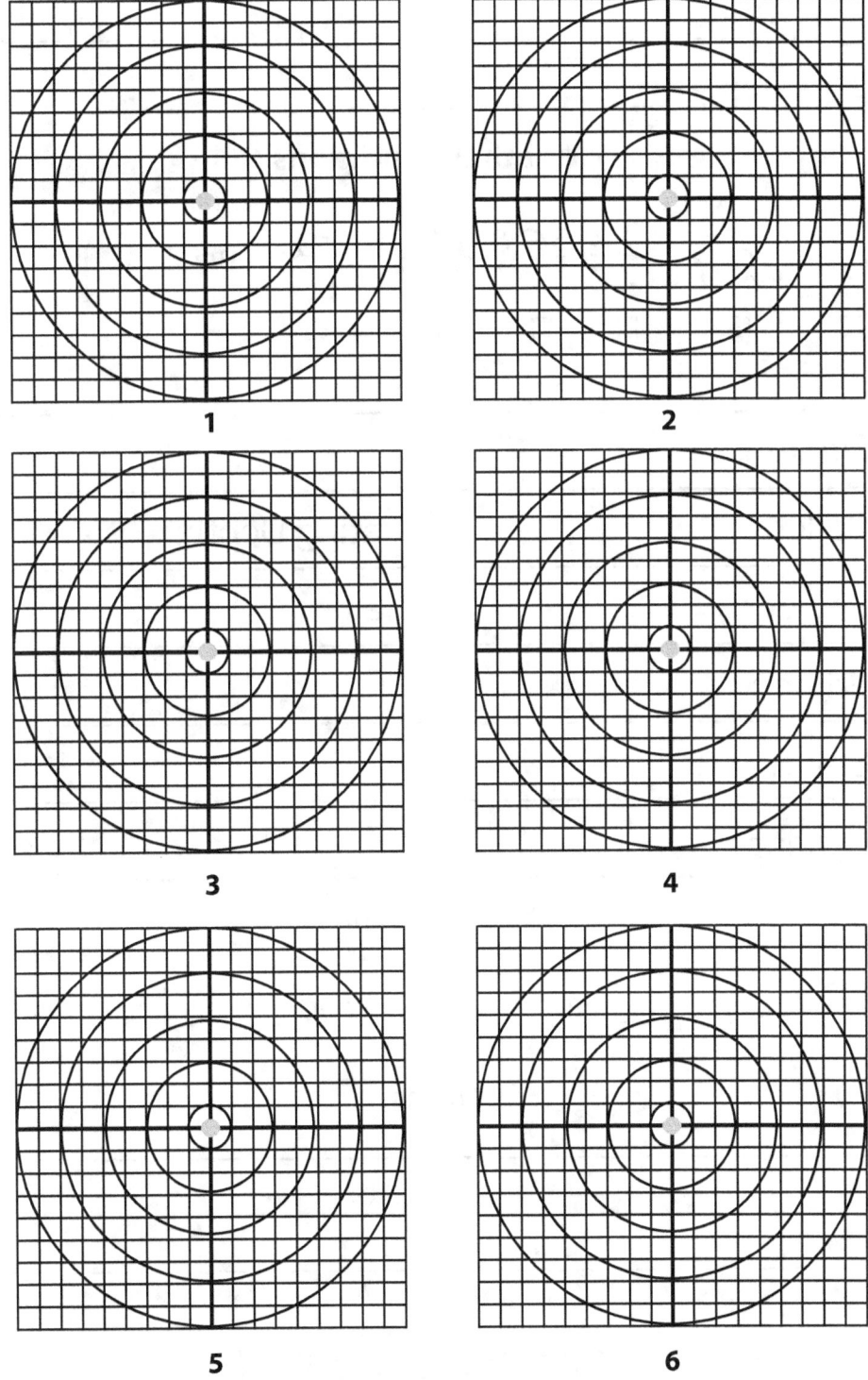

Date: _____ Time: _____

 Location: _____

Weather Conditions

☀ ☁ ⛅ 🌧 🌧 🌨 ⚑ 🌡
☐ ☐ ☐ ☐ ☐ ☐

Firearm:	
Bullet:	Seating Depth:
Powder:	Grains:
Primer:	
Brass:	
Distance:	

Overall Results

☐ Poor   ☐ Fair   ☐ Good   ☐ Excellent

Notes

_____
_____
_____

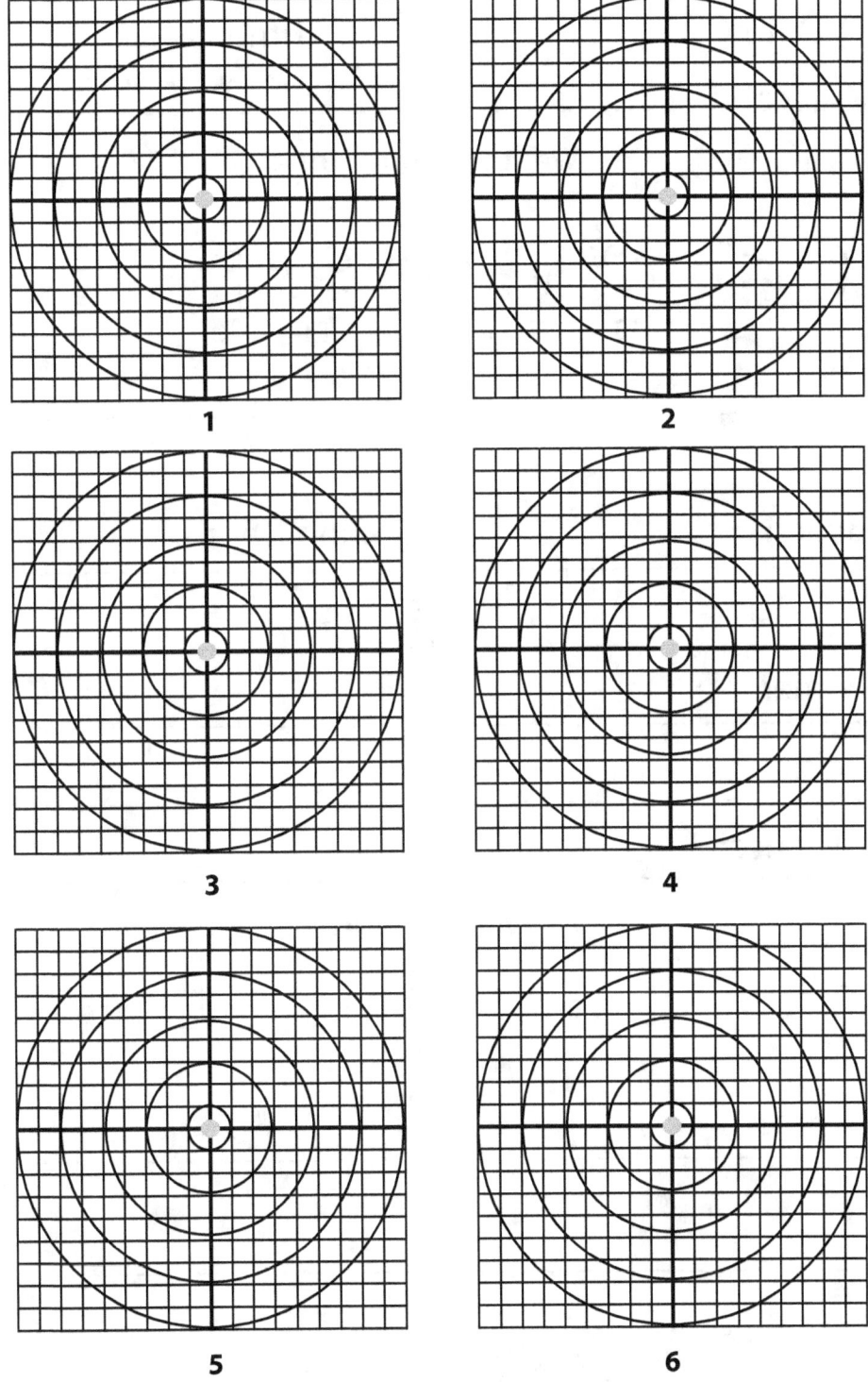

📅 Date: _____ 🕐 Time: _____

📍 Location: _____

Weather Conditions

☀️ ☁️ ⛅ 🌧️ 🌧️ 🌨️ 🚩 🌡️
☐ ☐ ☐ ☐ ☐ ☐ ___ ___

Firearm:	
Bullet:	Seating Depth:
Powder:	Grains:
Primer:	
Brass:	
Distance:	

Overall Results

☐ Poor   ☐ Fair   ☐ Good   ☐ Excellent

Notes

_____

_____

☆ ☆ ☆ ☆ ☆

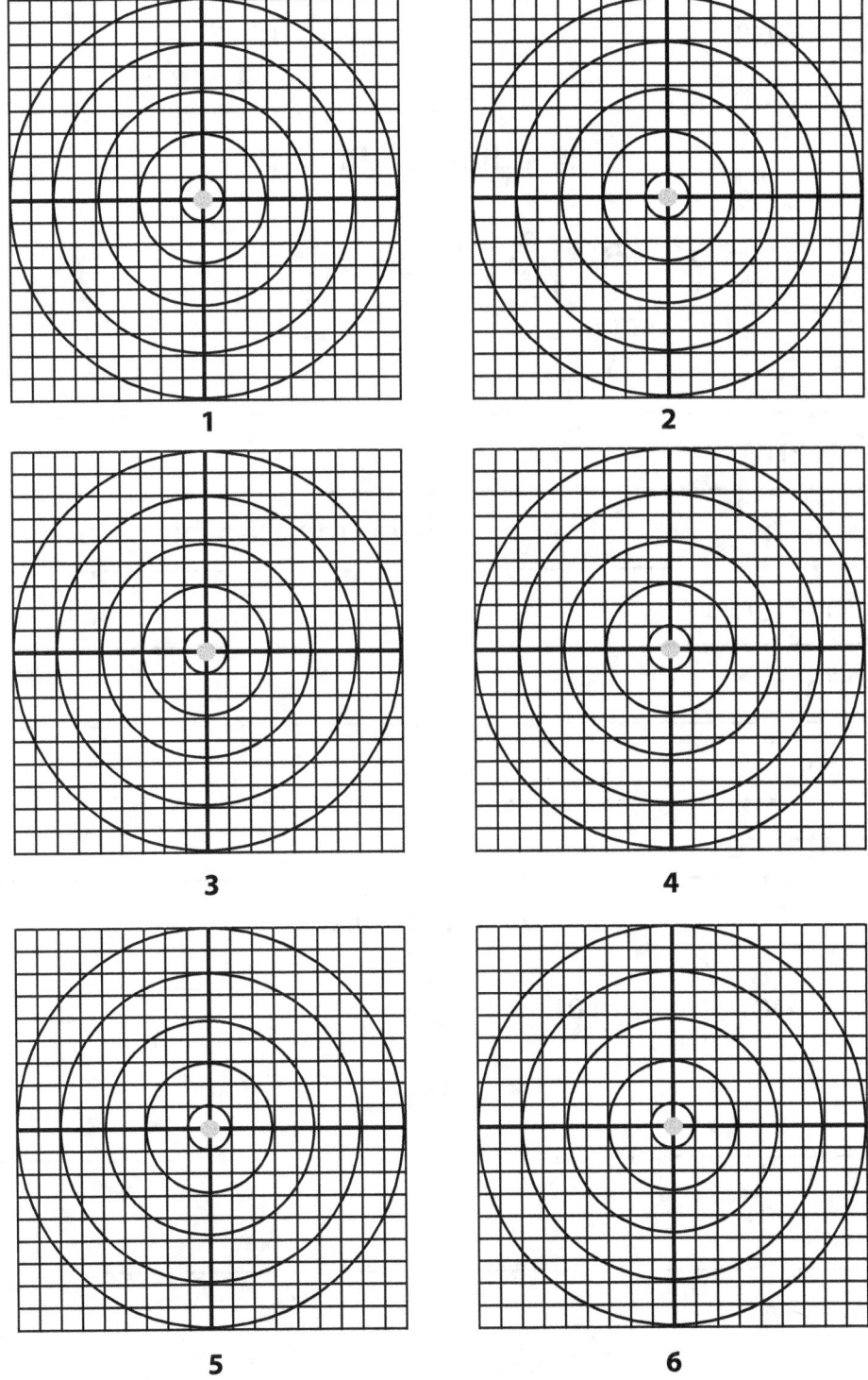

📅 Date: _____ 🕐 Time: _____

📍 Location: _____

Weather Conditions

☀ ☁ 🌥 🌧 🌧 🌨 🚩_____ 🌡_____
☐   ☐   ☐   ☐   ☐   ☐

Firearm:	
Bullet:	Seating Depth:
Powder:	Grains:
Primer:	
Brass:	
Distance:	

Overall Results

☐ Poor   ☐ Fair   ☐ Good   ☐ Excellent

Notes

_____
_____
_____

☆ ☆ ☆ ☆ ☆

www.ingramcontent.com/pod-product-compliance
Lightning Source LLC
Chambersburg PA
CBHW071125130526
44590CB00056B/2398